Keeping Out of Crime's Way

Keeping Out of Crime's Way ,

The Practical Guide for People Over 50 [by]

J. E. Persico with George Sunderland ,

An AARP Book
published by
American Association of Retired Persons   A. A. R. P. [c1985]
Washington, D.C.

Scott, Foresman and Company
Lifelong Learning Division
Glenview, Illinois

362.88

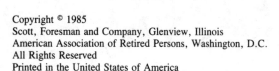

Library of Congress Cataloging in Publication Data

Persico, Joseph E.
  Keeping out of crime's way.

  Includes index.
  1. Aged—United States—Crimes against—Prevention.
  2. Crime prevention—United States—Citizen participation.
  3. Dwellings—United States—Security measures.
  I. Sunderland, George. II. Title.
  HV6250.4.A34P47   1985   362.8'8   84-24475
  ISBN 0-673-24801-1

Vacation Check-Off List (page 13), Property List (page 26), and Home Security Check-Off List (page 130) from *Crime Prevention Program,* 8th revision by George Sunderland. Reprinted by permission of the American Association of Retired Persons.

Checklist for Purchasing Alarm System (pages 22–23) from *Help Stop Crime,* published by the Dade County Public Safety Department, Dade County, Florida. Reprinted by permission.

12345678-KPF-908988878685

AARP Books is an educational and public service project of the American Association of Retired Persons, which, with a membership of more than 17 million, is the largest association of middle-aged and older persons in the world today. Founded in 1958, AARP provides older Americans with a wide range of membership programs and services, including legislative representation at both federal and state levels. For further information about additional association activities, write to AARP, 1909 K Street, N.W., Washington, DC 20049.

Contents

Acknowledgments

In the course of preparing *Keeping Out of Crime's Way: The Practical Guide for People Over 50,* numerous expert information sources were consulted. We particularly want to thank Lee Pearson of the Criminal Justice Services Section of the American Association of Retired Persons and Sergeant Frederick W. Ruckhaber of the Highland Park Police Department, Highland Park, Illinois, for their help and cooperation.

Introduction

Crime stands near the top of the list of matters that worry middle-aged or older Americans. Polls show crime ranking number two, exceeded only by income, as a concern of older people. Is that fear exaggerated? The answer, unfortunately, is no. The concern is thoroughly justified. In a typical year, one American household in three experiences a crime of theft or violence.

That is the bad news. *But there is good news too.* You, as a mid-life or older individual, can do a great deal to sharply reduce—and in some cases virtually eliminate—the likelihood that you will become a crime victim. That is the message of *Keeping Out of Crime's Way.*

The ticking clock of reported crimes committed in this country has by now become a cliché—a murder every twenty-five minutes, a rape every seven minutes, an armed robbery every fifty-nine seconds, a burglary every nine seconds, a theft every four seconds. These figures are beginning to leave us more numbed than shocked. Serious crime more than doubled during the 1960s. During the 1970s, crime kept climbing. Between 1960 and 1980, the U.S. population increased by 26 percent. At the same time, *reports of serious crime went up over 400 percent!* Only in 1982 was there any slight decline. But the crime rate remains intolerable.

Crime statistics are cold. They fail utterly to convey the pain and tragedy behind the numbers. A crime statistic is a terrified seventy-year-old widow who has moved rather than return to her burglarized apartment. A statistic is a sixty-six-year-old retired salesman whose desperately needed Social Security money for the month was taken in a robbery. It is an eighty-two-year-old woman rendered instantly destitute because she turned over her life savings to a con artist.

When crime does hit an older person, it hits especially hard. Suppose Peter, a middle-aged executive, has a net income of forty thousand dollars and loses four thousand dollars in a burglary, while Paul, a seventy-year-old pensioner with an income of four thousand dollars a year, loses four hundred dollars to a thief. Both suffered a 10 percent loss. Nevertheless, Peter still has thirty-six thousand dollars left to live on and can cut back on luxuries to absorb his loss. But Paul is already living close to the bone. His four-hundred-dollar loss has to be taken from the necessities of life.

Besides the financial cost, there is the psychological price that crime extracts from older Americans. A Pennsylvania study of older citizens revealed that one-quarter of them were afraid to be outside after school let out. Half of them did not dare leave home at night. Two-thirds of them would not open their doors to a stranger.

Given the pervasiveness of crime, people understandably despair that anything can be done about it. Many lose heart. A few years ago, the American Association of Retired Persons carried out a study of older persons living in the Dallas area. The study found that older citizens usually do not even bother to report crimes because they believe that the police will not or cannot do anything to help them.

The police cannot do much to prevent crime without the effort and involvement of individuals and communities. The police, for the most part, react to crimes already committed. And they are just one part of an overall inadequate criminal justice system. The police are overburdened. The courts are overloaded. And the prisons are overcrowded. Consequently, the odds favor the criminal at every step in the process. Most criminals are not caught. Most of those caught are not tried. Most of those tried are not convicted. Most of those convicted are not imprisoned. And most of those imprisoned do not serve their full sentences. Inmates are often released early—not because they are fit to return to society, but because there is no room for them in prison.

Today's older generation of Americans is understandably appalled by so much crime and the seeming inability of society to curb it. This generation went through the hardships of the Great Depression without nearly so much crime as occurs today. Its members lived through the stresses of a world war without the degree of lawlessness that the country is now experiencing.

What happened to create this sorry present state? Several forces have conspired to weaken the social fabric of the United States. Crime tends to be a game of the young. Consequently, crime soared as the postwar baby boom grew up. At the same time, numerous court decisions were enlarging the rights of criminals—often, it seemed, at the expense of innocent victims. Swift prosecution and sure punishment, according to criminologists, are the strongest deterrents against crime. Yet, today, it takes so long to bring a case to trial that the moral linkage between crime and punishment seems to be vanishing. A three-year lapse between the commission of a serious crime and imprisonment of the criminal is hardly unusual.

Finally, there has been the emergence of the drug culture and the crime it generates. A 1979 study of prison inmates showed that one-third of them were under the influence of drugs when they committed their crimes.

These changes, happening at roughly the same time—an increase in the young; the snaillike, sievelike nature of criminal justice; and a veritable explosion of illegal drug use—have bequeathed a crime-ridden society.

Of course, sociologists should continue to explore the roots of crime so that its social causes can be eliminated (though criminologists now largely confess their complete bafflement at the causes of crime).

Courts must be reformed so that they work better and more quickly. Reforms must be made in bail and parole policies so that dangerous people are not roaming the streets. The prison system must confine whoever ought to be confined—and for as long as the specific crime warrants. But, in the meantime, crime marches on. You cannot wait for society to find a cure for crime. You need protection here and now. The message of this book is that you are your own best protection. You can take individual action to shield yourself from many crimes.

The first step is to understand how crime affects older people. Older Americans do not necessarily suffer more or less crime than the general population. But they do experience more of certain crimes—burglaries and swindles, for example—than younger people. And they experience less of other crimes—crimes of violence, like homicide, rape, and aggravated assault—than young people. Someone between sixteen and twenty-four is eight times more likely to be a victim of violent crime than someone over sixty-five.

It is important to put crime against older people into this perspective. You need to know what the real dangers are so that you can take appropriate action. These, on the whole, are going to be crimes against your property. On the other hand, you need to be aware of the crimes of violence and what you can do to protect yourself. You need not be unnecessarily frightened over crimes that are far less likely to happen to you. The purpose of this book is to stress intelligent concern over paralyzing fear and to offer positive actions to replace helpless inertia.

In *Keeping Out of Crime's Way*, each major crime category is discussed in a separate chapter to give you a clear picture of what that crime is and to tell you what you can do to avoid becoming its victim. Virtually all of these tips are simple to take and are free or cost little money. Sometimes it is merely a matter of reminding you of commonsense protections. Burglaries in this country, for example, could be slashed by about 25 percent by one simple act. Lock your doors. In one burglary out of four, the thief merely walked through an unlocked door. Likewise, about half the victims of car theft were unwitting accomplices of the thief. They left a key in the ignition.

All of the precautions are simple, inexpensive ways to foil criminals. Most of them you can do yourself. In addition, you and your neighbors can band together to stop crime and outwit criminals.

You can indeed be your own best protection. You can stop certain crimes outright. And you can sharply reduce the occurrence of others. Instead of becoming a crime victim, you can keep out of crime's way.

1 Burglary

For Alma F. it promised to be a happy day. Alma, seventy-two, a widow, was flying that afternoon to California to visit her daughter, whom she had not seen for four years. More exciting, she was going to see her newest grandson, whom she had never seen at all. Alma was a self-sufficient woman. She knew that her daughter could not pay for her fare. So Alma had made sacrifices from her meager budget and had saved enough to pay her own way.

But at the last minute, something was still nagging at Alma, her old shoes. They were just not right for the handsome suit she had chosen for the trip. She left her house, and, because spring was at last in the air, she walked downtown. Luckily she found just what she wanted, though Alma felt a little guilty about spending the money. Still, she was going to give a substantial cash gift to her new grandson. That was Alma's tactful way of helping her daughter, who was just as proud as she was. Alma went home tired but exhilarated to wait for her brother, who was driving her to the airport.

When she got there, Alma felt an odd shudder. Her front door was slightly ajar. With her heart pounding, she went instantly to the kitchen table, where she had left the airline tickets. They were gone. So was the envelope with the cash for her grandson that she had hidden under her nightgown in the dresser.

It was not until later, after the police came, that she learned the full extent of her loss: her television set, the diamond engagement ring that her late husband had given her fifty years ago, and other treasured items.

She had been gone from the house for forty minutes during broad daylight. With a heavy heart, Alma started to dial her daughter. She was not coming to California after all.

Alma F. was the victim of a burglary. The Federal Bureau of Investigation (FBI) defines burglary as "unlawful entry of any fixed structure, vehicle, or vessel used for regular residence, industry, or business with or without force, with the intent to commit a felony or a larceny." Of all major crimes reported in the FBI Uniform Crime Reports, burglary heads the list. And burglary is one of the most frequent crimes that strike older persons. Why? For one thing, because so many older people live alone, which eases the burglar's job. And many older citizens live in low-rent areas, where the general crime level tends to be higher.

The sheer amount of burglary in this country is staggering. A burglary is committed somewhere in the United States every nine seconds. Residential burglaries have been increasing faster than business burglaries. Daytime burglaries have been increasing faster than nighttime burglaries. Yet many law-enforcement officers believe that *most burglaries can be prevented*.

Who is today's burglar? Most burglars are young. One recent study found that 64 percent of all burglars apprehended were under eighteen. A second major characteristic is that most burglars are not professionals. There are some slick second-story men and jewelry and art thieves both on television and in real life. But the overwhelming number of burglars might more accurately be called youthful opportunists. They look for easy opportunities to enter your house and steal. Their amateurism works in your favor. It is tough to thwart a skilled burglar, but you can often foil the others.

Most burglars do not want anything but your money or your goods. They want to get in and out as easily and quickly as possible. If the burglar is caught in the act, trapped, or scared, he or she might resort to violence. And some drug addicts, who commit a phenomenal amount of burglary, can be irrational or dangerous when confronted. But, for the most part, burglaries remain crimes of property and not of violence.

What the burglar wants is to get into your home easily. If the burglar was looking for tough challenges, he or she would take up another line of work. In about one burglary in three, the thief just enters through an unlocked door or window. A crime-prevention study over several months in St. Petersburg, Florida, showed that 63 percent of the time burglars entered homes through *unlocked* doors or doors with poor locks. Other common ways that burglars enter are through windows (often left unlocked); by finding keys "hidden" under doormats, in mailboxes, or other obvious places; by breaking a pane of glass in a door or window and opening it; by slipping, or pulling out, locks; by removing external hinge pins; by kicking in frail door panels; by forcing or prying doors open; and by lifting a sliding glass patio door off its tracks, forcing its flimsy locks, or prying the sliding door open.

Once inside, a burglar looks for money or anything that can easily be converted into cash. The burglar is an authority on where you have concealed your money. He or she knows all the favorite hiding places: under the clock on a mantel, in a chest of drawers, inside a sock, under a mattress, in the china closet— even in the freezer.

Besides cash, other high-target burglary items are jewelry, silver, credit cards, cameras, furs, television sets, home computers, stereos, tape recorders, typewriters, watches, coin collections, guns and gun collections, expensive bicycles, and anything portable and valuable that can easily be sold.

Alma F. was the victim of a young, opportunistic, unskilled burglar. She was only going out for a short while. She was staying in her neighborhood. It was broad daylight. And, so, she left the door unlocked. She left her plane tickets lying about exposed. And she hid her cash in an obvious place. A drug addict (it was later learned) had knocked on her door with some phony story in mind in case anyone answered. When no one did, he simply went through the unlocked door. He was out five minutes later.

There are professional burglars to worry about too. They operate quite differently.

Fred R. specializes in jewelry. He picks a time that most of us would consider relatively free of crime, Sunday morning. Fred parks his car across from an apartment building. He watches people going in and out—mostly to church, he rightly assumes. That means prolonged absences. He is sharp-eyed and takes note of when people leave or return. He then takes down several names from mailboxes in the apartment house foyer. He later gets the phone numbers of these people from the phone book.

The following Sunday Fred again parks near the apartment house. From a nearby pay phone he starts calling from his list until he gets a "no answer." He gambles that he has reached the apartment of someone out to church. That gives Fred considerable time to operate. He takes out an attaché case (he is neatly dressed in a jacket and tie). He enters the apartment house and slips the lock on the empty apartment. (Fred's a pro.) He leaves with $250 in cash and $3,000 in jewelry.

You have now seen two kinds of burglars in action: the unskilled opportunist and the polished thief. They may strike during the night while you are asleep or during the day while you shop or when you are off on vacation. But, according to law-enforcement authorities, *most burglaries can be prevented.*

Protection While You Are Away

The most vulnerable time for burglary is when you are away from home for an extended period—a few days or even a few weeks. There stands your home, empty and unprotected. It is evening. The burglar is cruising through a neighborhood. He passes a white, two-story colonial house and spots several newspapers on the porch. The house is pitch dark. He parks his car and approaches the house. He notices that the grass needs cutting. He finds the mailbox stuffed with mail. There is a note taped to the door: "Frank, mower in garage. Help self. Needs gas." This house is empty, and he can work it at his leisure.

The Lived-In Look

The best protection against burglars when you go away for any length of time is to make your home *appear* occupied. The first thing to do is get rid of those telltale clues, the piled-up newspapers and the stuffed mailbox. You may decide to call the newspaper and ask them to stop delivering during your absence. You can tell the post office to hold your mail. But have you followed the wisest course? Maybe you had no alternative. But just by turning off these deliveries, you have informed maybe a half-dozen people—most of them strangers—who you are, where you live, and when you are going to be away.

There is a far better alternative, assuming it is available to you—your neighbors. Ask a trusted neighbor to pick up your newspapers and mail while you are gone. Ask your neighbors to keep an eye on your home generally and to report anything suspicious to the police. Nosy neighbors may be a pain when you are at home, but they can be a protection when you are away. It is also a good idea to let a neighbor know where you can be reached in case of emergencies. Caution neighbors not to tell strangers such as salespeople and repair persons of your absence.

The absence of an automobile is another tip-off that a house may be vacant. You might arrange with your neighbor to leave a car parked in your driveway or in front of your house while you are gone. If you keep your car in a garage that has windows, place shades on those windows to prevent anyone from looking in to see whether a car is present.

Then, make arrangements to have your lawn mowed during your absence or your walk and driveway shoveled if it is winter.

It is also a good idea to adjust blinds and draperies to make the house or apartment appear to be occupied.

House-Sitters

The best way to make your house look lived in is to *have it lived in.* Try to arrange for a house-sitter while you are gone. A son or daughter, a grown grandchild, or a trusted friend might be willing to move in temporarily. You can even contact professional house-sitter services. Often sitters can be arranged through college placement offices that will find students or even faculty members to stay in your home.

Your Dog

Should your dog be lodged with family or friends or at a boarding kennel while you are gone? If possible, have a friend or neighbor feed your dog at home and walk him. A dog's bark is an unwelcome sound to a burglar's ear.

Lights On

Many of us have a lifelong aversion to leaving lights on in an empty room, but lights suggest an occupied home. And compare the cost of a few kilowatts of power to the loss, for example, of your silverware. So, if you are going to be away, leave a few lights on in strategic places. A good idea is to leave a bathroom light on and a door slightly ajar. This suggests that someone has gotten up in the middle of the night and is using the bathroom.

A house ablaze with lights in the middle of the night may give a burglar the opposite signal from what you intended. It says, "Hey, look, we're not home. But we're trying to look as if we are." There is a simple, inexpensive answer to that quandary—the electric timer. Such a timer can be connected to a light in your bedroom, for example, so that the light goes on at 8:00 P.M. and off at midnight. Or, if the glow of a television screen is a familiar sign that you are in, you can also connect the timer to your television set. Since lights going on and off at exactly the same time every night may signal to a thief that no one is home, you may want to buy inexpensive timers that will vary the on-off times.

Radios

Another good idea is to leave a radio on loud enough so that it can be heard from just outside your doorway. All-talk stations are particularly good. If the burglar doesn't tarry too long, he or she may mistake the voices for conversation and move on.

Telephones

What about the telephone? Some people leave the telephone off the hook when they are going to be away. The idea is that a burglar may phone first to see if anyone is home, and a busy signal tells the burglar that someone is. But the experts, both in crime prevention and at the telephone company, say a phone off the hook is not a good idea. If the line is always busy, it may send an opposite message to the burglar—that no one is in the house. Also, leaving the phone off the hook ties up equipment and can generate misleading out-of-order reports. However, there is one thing you can do with your phone to discourage intruders—set the tone down so that the ringing cannot be heard from the outside. Repeated rings signal that no one is answering and, therefore, the house is empty.

House Keys

Do not hide your house key anywhere on the outside of the house—under the doormat, over the doorsill, or in the mailbox. Do not keep any form of identification on your key chain. If you lose the keys, it is far better to have them replaced than to have the wrong party find the keys—along with the address of the house where the keys fit.

Separate your house keys from your car keys when you park in a place that requires you to leave the key in the car. It is easy for someone to find your address from your car registration or perhaps from a piece of mail left in your car. If you have left the house keys in the car, someone can quickly and easily get the keys duplicated and thus be able to get into your house.

Garage Doors and Windows

Attached garages offer burglars a wonderful cover for breaking into your house. If the garage door is unlocked, the thief need merely close it behind him or her. Now the thief can work on opening the door into the house in total privacy. He or she may even find the tools in the garage to ease the job. Always lock your garage door just as you do the doors to your house. The same holds true with garage windows. Also, remove any ladders from sight and secure them *inside* the garage or in another locked place.

Locking Up Your Valuables

Recognizing that, despite your best efforts, your home may still be burglarized while you are gone, leave the burglar less to take. Do not leave cash, checks, or securities in the house. There is hardly a hiding place that you can imagine that burglars have not already thought about. Put your jewelry and other valuables in a safe-deposit box. Lock up other items in a secure room—things like furs, cameras, and silver. In other words, make your house less profitable for the criminal.

If you must keep valuables in the house, a home safe is a good idea. But remember that the burglar may carry away the safe and all. So have your home safe securely mounted to the wall or floor in some not easily accessible place.

Don't Advertise Your Absence

Your departure for business or pleasure may be considered newsworthy in your community. If so, keep the news to yourself, at least until you get back. A news note to the effect that Mr. and Mrs. Higby will be visiting their son who lives in Washington is also an advertisement that the Higby house is about to become an easy mark.

Let the Police Know

Finally, always notify your local police when you are going to be away for any period. They quite likely will be able to check your home from time to time. Nothing is less encouraging to burglary than the sight of a squad car. Let the police know who among your neighbors or friends may be looking after your house. This information could avoid an embarrassing case of seeming illegal entry.

Home Security

Some, but not all, of the precautions discussed earlier apply even if you are going to be out of your home for a short time. Rule Number One: Always lock your doors. Lock the door even if you live in an apartment house and are just going down the hall to dispose of trash. Leaving the radio on is advised for short absences too. Leave some lights on if you are going out for the evening. And don't leave a spare key hidden outside the house or apartment.

Home security, of course, involves more than the precautions taken to avoid burglary during a short- or long-term absence.

VACATION CHECK-OFF LIST

Check

1. Lock all doors, including the garage door. . . . . ☐

2. Lock all windows, including basement and garage windows. . . . . ☐

3. Cancel all deliveries such as newspapers and milk. . . . . ☐

4. Have mail and newspapers picked up by a neighbor if possible. . . . . ☐

5. Have someone pick up handbills and throwaways. . . . . ☐

6. Never leave a note on the door that may indicate your absence. . . . . ☐

7. Arrange to have the lawn cut or the snow shoveled. . . . . . . ☐

8. Adjust blinds and draperies to make the house or apartment appear to be occupied. . . . . ☐

9. Place a light or two on automatic timers. . . . . ☐

10. Remove ladders from sight and secure them in locked places. . . . . ☐

11. Don't hide keys under doormats or flowerpots or in similar places. . . . . ☐

12. Secure items such as jewelry, furs, cameras, credit cards, and checkbooks. . . . . ☐

13. Arrange for a house-sitter, someone to live in your house while you are away, if possible. . . . . ☐

14. Arrange for a neighbor to keep an eye on your property and to report anything suspicious to police. . . . . ☐

15. Let a neighbor know where you can be reached in case of an emergency. . . . . ☐

16. Arrange with a neighbor to leave his or her car parked in your driveway or in front of your house or apartment. . . . . ☐

17. Leave a radio on just inside your doorway. . . . . ☐

18. Lower the tone on your telephone. ☐

19. Ask neighbors not to tell strangers such as salespersons and repair persons of your absence. . . . . ☐

20. Do not advertise your absence in the local social notices. . . ☐

21. Notify your local law-enforcement agency of your absence. . . . . ☐

Telephone Tricks

Professional burglars are full of tricks to find out which homes are empty. They will even check the obituary columns to find out when survivors are liable to be at a funeral service.

Here is another such scam. Suppose you get a phone call. "Hi, Mrs. Callan. I'm Joann Horton of Glamour Line. We're test-marketing our new hair conditioner in your neighborhood next week. We'd like to send our representative to drop off some free samples for you. Please tell us if you are going to be out at any time. We would hate to miss you. And people take the samples if we leave them outside."

The caller may be legitimate. But, Joann may also be a shrewd thief trying to find out when your home will be empty so that it can be burglarized. Never, under any circumstances, tell a stranger when you won't be in.

Doors

Doors provide the easiest access to your home. If you live in a house, any interior basement door as well as any interior entranceway door to a garage must be considered vulnerable.

If you live in an apartment, particularly in an older building, your door may have easily removed decorative paneling. If so, try to have your landlord secure the inside of that door with a back-up sheet of steel or good solid plywood.

Your outside-door locks are your first line of defense. What kind of an obstacle do your locks present to a burglar?

Spring-latch lock.   Does your front door, for example, have an easy-to-open spring latch? That is simple enough to determine. Open the door. Is there a beveled end on the bolt? Can you push the bolt back into the door by pressing against the beveled part? If so, you have a spring-latch lock. And it is a cinch for a burglar. He or she can probably open your door simply by inserting something thin and stiff, like a credit card or a knife blade, into the space between the door and the frame. The pressure against that beveled edge of the bolt will unlock your door.

A spring-latch lock is illustrated in figure 1.

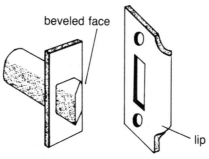

Fig. 1. Spring bolt and strike

Thumb-turn dead-bolt lock.   A far more secure device is the dead-bolt lock. The dead-bolt lock has a squarish bolt with no spring and no beveled edge. Therefore the bolt cannot be pushed open as described above. If the bolt is long enough, say an inch and a half, it also becomes difficult to jimmy the door open. The strike plate should be anchored properly with three-inch screws. The dead-bolt lock is the most burglarproof lock available. It belongs on all your outside doors. This lock is shown in figure 2. Dead-bolt locks may be operated by thumb turns or keys.

Double-cylinder lock.   But suppose you have a window in the door? Homes often do. It makes the door attractive. What is to prevent the burglar from smashing a pane or cutting away some

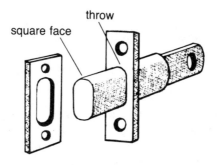

Fig. 2. Dead-bolt lock and strike

glass, reaching in, and opening the door from the inside—even a door locked with a dead bolt? One answer here is the double-cylinder lock. Such a lock has to be unlocked by a key from the inside as well as from the outside. In other words, should the burglar knock out a pane and reach inside to a double-cylinder lock, he or she still could not open the door. You have nicely inconvenienced a thief who is trying to make the burglary as simple as possible—and who may move on to easier pickings.

But there is a disadvantage to the double-cylinder lock. In case of a fire or other emergency, you would have to unlock your door before you could get out of the house. Some jurisdictions recognize this danger and have prohibited the use of double-cylinder locks. But if they are legal where you live and you want their considerable protection, keep a key inside where you can get to it in a hurry.

An alternative is to replace the windowpane with burglar-resistant laminated glass having a .060-inch polyvinyl butyral (PVB) interlayer.

Chain lock.   What about a chain lock? It seems like such a sensible device. A chain lock allows you to open the door just enough to see who is out there, without opening it enough to let an unwanted visitor in. Also, on the plus side, a chain lock tells a burglar that someone is at home. Nevertheless, a chain lock is not going to keep out a determined thief. A shoulder thrust against the door will pull a chain lock off the door frame. So if you do use a chain lock, make sure that it is secured with good long screws.

Peephole.   Preferable to the chain lock and serving a similar purpose is the peephole. The best peepholes have a wide-angle lens that gives you a good view outside the door. Solid outside doors, particularly those in apartments, should always have peepholes, or door viewers.

Sliding door.   The attractive sliding glass patio door is also attractive to burglars. Sliding doors can sometimes be lifted from their tracks. Usually their locks are not strong and are easily forced. But there are simple ways to make your sliding glass door more secure. Just place a stick, something like a dowel or broomstick handle, in the track. That jams the track, and the door cannot be slid back. And pins inserted through the track and into the door will also prevent lifting the door from its track. These techniques are illustrated in figures 3 and 4.

Fig. 3. Broom handle blocking sliding door

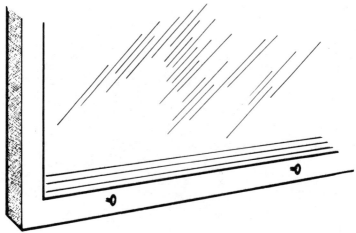

Fig. 4. Pins preventing lifting of sliding door

Windows

The burglar's second favorite means of entry, after the door, is the window. Over 90 percent of residential burglaries are committed through doors or windows. About a third of these occur through windows. And a third of the time the windows are not locked! Keep your windows locked at all times when they do not have to be open. Again, the burglar can break or cut the glass to open a window lock. If desperate enough, the intruder could smash out the whole window to gain entry. More often than not, he or she will choose a quieter way. The burglar does not want to arouse suspicion by creating noise and is not eager to clamber through a window frame of jagged glass.

Double-hung windows, the kind where you push the bottom half up and the top half down, can be opened even if secured by butterfly locks, which you twist into place. These are the locks that are commonly found on double-hung windows. See figure 5. Butterfly locks can sometimes be opened by sliding something thin and rigid, like a credit card or knife blade, through the crack between the top and bottom windows. This approach can be thwarted, if you are willing to spend the money, by installing key-operated window locks. See figure 6. Such locks, however, present a fire hazard if the window is the only escape route and you have to take time to locate a key.

But there is a less expensive, easier window protection. Just drill a quarter-inch hole into the window frame on each side of the window. Then put a metal pin or a large nail into the hole, leaving one-quarter inch exposed so the pin or nail can be

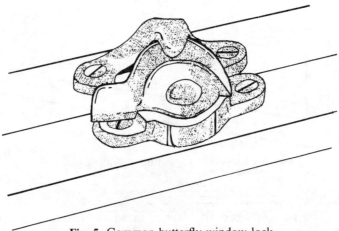

Fig. 5. Common butterfly window lock

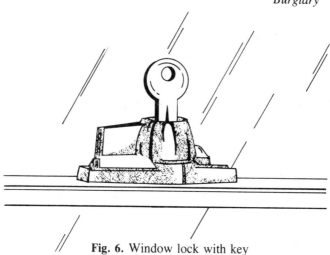

Fig. 6. Window lock with key

removed quickly and easily. The pin or nail will now prevent the window from being raised all the way. Additional holes can be drilled at different levels to allow for adjustments in ventilation while still keeping the window secured. If you are unable to do the drilling, ask a neighbor or relative. It is a simple procedure. See figure 7.

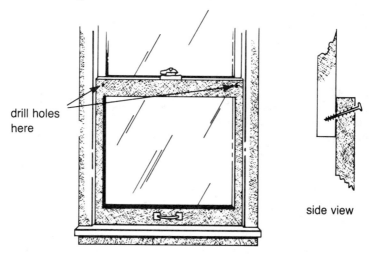

drill holes here

side view

Fig. 7. Pinning double-hung windows

Air Conditioners

Burglars may consider another means of entry to your home. What about the air conditioner that is installed in your window? If it can be removed, the burglar not only gains easy entry but also gets an air conditioner as the first part of the loot. The remedy here is to secure window air-conditioning units with long screws or bolts fitted into the window and the house or apartment.

Outside Lighting

Darkness is the nighttime burglar's friend. By the same token, adequate, well-placed lighting outside your home can discourage thieves. Public street lighting may be adequate. Streetlights are one of the best investments in crime prevention that your community can make. The way one police chief put it, "A good streetlight is almost as valuable as a good policeman, and a lot cheaper."

But, if you live on a dark street or in a secluded area, you should take protective action yourself. You want just enough light to expose unwanted visitors, without annoying your neighbors. Here is a good test. Walk around your house after dark. If you can read your watch, the area is adequately illuminated. If not, you should install some lighting.

Places that particularly should be lit are doorways and windows. Ideally, you should have spotlights placed on each corner of your house. But two lights on opposite corners may do the trick almost as well. Whatever outside lights you use, be sure to protect each bulb so that it cannot simply be broken or unscrewed by a burglar. Vandal-proof covers can be purchased at many hardware and lighting stores. Light makes it tougher for the prospective intruder to escape the eyes of your neighbors, passersby, and patrolling police.

Exterior lighting can be placed on a timer, which can be adjusted to the changing seasons.

Lighting for security purposes need not be unattractive. Done with taste, lighting can improve the beauty of your property. Note how often buildings and statuary are enhanced by tasteful lighting arrangements. The ideal positioning for home-security lighting is shown in figure 8.

Fig. 8. Exterior home lighting

Shrubs and Hedges

Everybody appreciates a well-landscaped home. But bushes, shrubs, and hedges may help make the burglar's job easier. A pair of full arborvitae flanking the front door may be handsome. The trees also offer concealment to a would-be burglar. The same goes for hedges and shrubs around the house and particularly in front of cellar windows. A bush may offer perfect concealment while a burglar pries open a window leading to your cellar.

You do not, however, have to give up the beauty of landscaping in your efforts to minimize the danger from crime. Just design your greenery wisely to minimize opportunities for intruders to hide. And keep your hedges, bushes, and shrubs trimmed to heights that do not offer much concealment. As a rule, never let foliage grow past the bottom ledge of any window and never let it obscure an entranceway door.

Alarms

Should you have a household burglar alarm? It depends on what type protection you want and what you are willing to pay. Home alarms run the gamut in sophistication and price. The simplest and probably least expensive is a battery-operated door alarm. It requires no wiring. You merely install it and turn it on. The alarm sounds if the door is opened.

The variety of burglar alarms seems limited only by human imagination. You can buy an alarm that throws a beam of light between two points. It goes off when someone passes between those points. You can buy an ultrasonic alarm that detects motion in a room; or a pressure mat that fits under a carpet and sounds an alarm when someone steps on it; or sensors that detect the breaking of glass, or vibrations, or even fingers touching a home safe.

Home security has become a growth industry in this country. You can no doubt find retailers, such as hardware stores, selling alarm systems in your area. They make sense. And you can find something in almost every price range. A helpful checklist for buying an alarm is given below. Be sure to check on local ordinances and codes before making your purchase.

CHECKLIST FOR PURCHASING ALARM SYSTEM

	Yes	No
1. Is the company a local business?		
2. Is repair service readily available?		
3. Is there a warranty or maintenance contract?		
4. Is the company a member of any local business or merchants' organization?		
5. If it is, did you check with the organization for length of time in business and past performance?		
6. Is the system operated electrically or by battery? If electrically operated, does it switch automatically to battery power without activating the alarm in the event of a power failure?		
7. If the alarm system is activated, will it automatically shut off after a reasonable alert period (10–15 minutes)?		
8. After the system is activated, will it automatically reset if attacked again?		

CHECKLIST FOR PURCHASING ALARM SYSTEM *(continued)*

Yes No

	Yes	No
9. If the control switch or box is exposed, will it activate the alert if attacked?		
10. If it is a hardwire system (wires connecting sensor to control to alert), are the wires protected from attack and unnecessary wear by the elements?		
11. If it is a local system (audible in the immediate area), does it ring loud enough to attract the attention of your neighbors?		
12. If the system is for a commercial premise, will the company have someone respond to the location in order to assist the police by opening the building?		
13. Does the system have time delay, if appropriate, to activate and deactivate the alarm system without setting off the alert?		
14. If the system is monitored by a central station, is it a tape recording or person? Check with your local law-enforcement agency on its requirements for answering a report coming through an alarm system.		
15. Is the entire system Underwriters Laboratories, Inc. (U.L.) approved?		
16. Does the alarm company provide decals so you can advertise your security system and thus deter a burglar?		
17. Is the system up to local codes and ordinances?		
18. Is the alarm company licensed, by the municipality or the state?		

Confronting a Burglar

Let us assume the worst. You have been burglarized, and you actually encounter the burglar. If you should come home and see any sign of improper entry—a door or window forced open, for example—*do not enter your house.* Go immediately to a neighbor's, if practical, and call the police. Then wait until the police arrive to check out your house before you go in. The last thing you want is a physical confrontation with a criminal. Let the police do the work that they are trained to perform.

But a burglary may take place while you are in the house. Say it is nighttime. You are in bed. You hear a noise and go to investigate. You confront the burglar. Keep this in mind: *What you want to save first is your life.* Property comes in a distant second. Bear in mind that what the burglar wants most is to escape. So do not confront the intruder. Do not enter further into the room where you found the thief. Give him (the likelihood of confronting a female is remote) space to get out. The more the burglar senses that he is trapped, the more likely the intruder is to resort to violence. Humans, like animals, respond defensively to intrusions into their space. Psychologists have a phrase for this phenomenon. They call it the idea of "critical distance." Critical distance is that borderline space that separates the instinct to flee from the instinct to fight. Research has shown that when police officers are killed in the line of duty, in three out of four such cases the officer placed himself within ten feet of his assailant. So don't invade the burglar's critical distance. You want yourself and your loved ones safe. And you want the burglar out of your house. Don't stand in his way.

Weapons

Guns are found in about half the homes in the United States. Many are hunting weapons. Some are used for target shooting. Others are collectors' items. But many are handguns intended for personal protection. Should you keep a handgun in your home for security? That question raises several others: Is the weapon legal? Do you know how to use it safely? Do you know the legal implications of using that weapon?

In a typical year, as many as twenty-five thousand Americans die from gunshot wounds. About half of these deaths occur in or around the home, and many of them result from tragic accidents. Someone roused from a sound sleep may sense a furtive movement and shoot an innocent person, even a family member. And suppose your weapon is wrested from you by an intruder? The gun you keep for protection may be more dangerous to you than the criminal. Most law-enforcement officers advise against keeping a handgun in the house, even if you have obtained it legally. The risk is just too great.

Reclamation of Property

Picture a room in your home, say the dining room. Write down everything in it. Then take your list into the room and see how many items you actually remembered. What about the heirloom silver candelabra you put in that drawer in the china closet two years ago? Was that on your list?

Without an inventory of your property so that you can determine what is missing, you cannot hope to reclaim everything that might be taken in a burglary. Also, property should be marked or photographed for ready identification.

Inventorying Your Property

If you are burglarized, you are probably not going to remember everything that may have been stolen. Take the time to draw up a personal property inventory. Keep the completed list in a secure place, such as a safe-deposit box. Not only will the list be useful to the police if you are burglarized, but it will also help you in making your insurance claim. On page 26 is a model property inventory form that you can use.

Marking Your Property

Some years ago, the police chief of Monterey Park, California, came up with a clever antitheft program. His approach involved having people mark their personal property, usually with an electric etching tool. When you put your initials or an identifying number on your television set, camera, or other valuable property, you gain four ways. First, a thief is more likely to pass up an item that can be identified as stolen because he or she will have a tougher time selling it. Second, the police can more easily trace the owner of recovered stolen property if it has been marked. Third, you will have an easier time proving that the marked property is yours. Fourth, your marked property provides valuable evidence linking the culprit to the crime in a trial.

Marking your property is probably going to cost you nothing. Usually the electric etching tool is loaned out by police or

PROPERTY LIST

	Item and Make	Serial Number	Personal Identification Number	Original Cost
Radio				
Stereo				
Tape Recorder				
Television				
Power Tools				
Special Equipment				
Dryer				
Washer				
Other Appliances				
Binoculars				
Cameras				
Jewelry				
Watches				
Sewing Machine				
Sporting Goods				
Typewriter				

	Item and Make	Color	License Number	Personal Identification Number	Original Cost
Automobile					
Motorcycle					
Scooter					
Bicycle					
Lawn Mower					

	Make	Serial Number	Caliber	Personal Identification Number	Original Cost
Guns					

other community agencies for short periods free of charge. Often the etching tools are placed in convenient locations, such as libraries and fire stations, from which you can borrow them.

Some police departments in the marking program will give you a sticker to place on your door or window showing that your property has been marked. That sticker can deter a burglar. You may want to photograph items like jewelry, furs, and antiques, which cannot or should not be marked for identification.

Don't Be Struck Twice

Lightning is not supposed to strike the same place twice. But burglars do. If you have already been burglarized once, you can expect another attempt. If entry was through a locked door, *have your locks changed.*

DON'TS AND DOS

Don't
- leave doors and windows unlocked.
- leave messages on the door while you are away.
- hide door keys under doormats, in mailboxes, or in other obvious places outside the house or apartment.
- leave money and valuables around your home when you go away.
- allow newspapers, mail, or circulars to accumulate in front of your door while you are away.
- put notices in newspapers or other publications announcing that you are going away.
- leave the phone off the hook while you are away.
- have your address on your key ring.
- leave your house keys in your car when you park commercially.
- be lured from your home by ruses.
- depend on a handgun for burglary protection.
- threaten or confront a burglar.

Do

- have a neighbor or friend pick up your newspapers, mail, and other delivered material when you go away.
- ask neighbors to keep an eye on your home while you are away.
- notify the police if you are going to be away for long periods.
- leave certain lights on when you go away. Connect them to an automatic timer.
- leave on your radio when you are out of the home.
- arrange to have your lawn mowed or snow shoveled.
- have someone look after your dog at home when you go away.
- arrange for a house-sitter, if practical.
- secure your windows with metal pins.
- install dead-bolt locks on your doors.
- report any criminal activity or suspicious behavior.
- consider installing a burglar-alarm system.
- mark your property with an electric etching tool.
- inventory your property—*before* you are burglarized.
- install security lighting outside your home.
- keep hedges and shrubs trimmed and not too tall.

Remember, above all, what the law-enforcement people tell us—
most burglaries can be prevented.

2 Robbery and Other Street Crimes

Harry G., eighty-two, looked forward to those hours at the hardware store. He had built the business from scratch. Now, he had pretty much turned the store over to his two grown sons. Still, Harry liked to put in a few hours every day. That night, a Thursday, the store closed at ten o'clock. At nine o'clock Harry started to feel a little tired. "Do you boys think you can handle this without me?" he had said. He had caught one son winking at the other as he said, "Sure, Dad."

On the way to his car, Harry passed by Feldman's Bakery, which was just getting ready to close. He stopped in to pick up a coffee cake for breakfast. His wife, Rose, loved coffee cake.

Harry started up Fulton Street. He had parked his car in the next block. The street was dark and empty except for a young fellow and a girl leaning against the window of the closed one-hour dry-cleaning shop. As Harry passed them, he felt something hard in his back—then a menacing whisper. "Keep moving, Pops, or you're a dead man." The young fellow shoved him into an alleyway. "Shut up. Do as you're told, and you won't get hurt," he said.

Harry could see the streetlight gleam on a pistol barrel. "You'll get nothing from me, punk," Harry said. Harry was a feisty guy. He was more angry than scared. Then the butt of the pistol crashed against his head.

The last thing that Harry remembered was the girl going through his pockets while the young fellow stood watch at the alley entrance. Then Harry passed out. The thieves had taken from him $289 in cash, his watch, a ring, and a dividend check.

When Harry's sons found him, he was still unconscious. Beside him was the smashed bakery box with the coffee cake. At the emergency room, they found that Harry had suffered a concussion.

Robbery

Harry G. was the victim of a robbery. The FBI defines robbery as "the taking or attempting to take anything of value from the care, custody, or control of a person by force or threat of force or violence and/or by putting the victim in fear."

Robbery is a nightmare come true, filled with the potential not only for material loss but also for violence and injury. And it happens with appalling frequency. According to the national crime survey 1,381,000 robberies were committed in one recent year. They run the range from big jobs—bank holdups, for example—to a child pinned against a wall in a schoolyard while another child relieves him of his lunch money. Robbery makes up about 40 percent of all crimes of violence. In half the cases, the robbers use force, and guns are used in about 40 percent of all robberies. Harry was the victim of a particular type of armed robbery and assault.

For whatever statistical consolation it offers, older people are less likely to be robbed than younger people—not because of age per se but because, out of fear, older persons do not venture out as frequently as younger persons. For every thousand persons aged twenty to twenty-four, about nine will be robbed in a typical year. For people sixty-five and older, that figure is about three and a half robberies per thousand. Robberies also tend to be a city crime. For every thousand people living in the central city, about twelve will be robbed. In the suburbs, that figure drops to just under five per thousand. In small towns or rural areas, the number of robbery victims drops further to about two and a half per thousand.

Who robs? To an overwhelming degree, the robber is a

young male. Robbery is a crime of violence, and 90 percent of violent crimes are committed by males, 30 percent of whom are under age nineteen. Seventy-two percent of them are under thirty. Few robbers are women. Only about seven of every hundred persons arrested for robbery in a recent typical year were female.

While robbery may happen more frequently to younger than older victims, it is a terrifying experience at any age. It also happens swiftly and rather randomly. Consequently, one tends to think that little can be done to avoid a robbery. Most robberies, something like 40 percent, are never even reported to the police. People, particularly in high-crime areas, come to feel that little can be done to stop robberies and that less can be done to recover their losses. But plenty can be done.

Preventive Measures to Take

What is the robber after, and how does he go about getting it? Above all, he wants your money and your valuables. He wants to get them as easily and as fast as possible. He wants to do so quickly to avoid being detected and caught. The easiest mark is someone alone. And the best place is somewhere dark and relatively deserted. These are the clues to preventing robbery.

First of all, do not go out alone at night if you can avoid it. You are much safer during daylight. And, day or night, it is always best to have a companion along. Stick to well-lighted streets where there are people. Don't try to save time by using shortcuts through alleyways, schoolyards, and parking lots.

It is even important where you walk on the sidewalk. A mugger is liable to conceal himself in a doorway, in an alleyway, or between parked cars. So it's best to use the middle of the sidewalk.

If you come upon a group of loiterers, particularly young men, cross the street. If you approach a parked car that is occupied and has the motor running and people in it, play it safe and cross the street.

Don't let strangers engage you in conversation.

Keep on moving. It is always a good idea to maintain a brisk, determined pace. Walk as though you are in a hurry and know where you are going.

If you think you are being followed, or if someone approaches you suspiciously, head for light and life. Move toward a well-lighted area. Head for people. Go into a store. Do not head directly for home, though that may be your natural impulse. You may be trapped in your doorway or alone in your elevator. You are better off on the street, where people can see you and where you can get help.

Traveling Light

Despite what you may do to avoid being robbed, you can still become a victim. However, should you be robbed, your losses can be minimized, and injury can be prevented.

One thing is certain. You cannot lose more than you are carrying. So, don't go around with large amounts of money. Carry only what you need for a particular outing. On the other hand, it is wise to carry at least enough money to appease a potential robber. You don't want a vicious thug or desperate addict attacking you because you were an unprofitable victim. And, always make sure that you have a few coins in case you have to make an emergency phone call.

Whatever money you do carry is best divided up. Don't keep everything in a purse or billfold. Tuck some into a pocket, a shoe, or even a bra.

One way to cut down on the amount of cash you carry is not to pay cash for your purchases. Pay by credit card or charge account or write a check. If possible, carry only the credit cards you intend to use and the exact number of checks you intend to write.

Should You Resist?

Let's imagine that, like Harry G., you find yourself looking at the barrel of a gun or at a knife or are otherwise threatened in the course of a robbery. Harry did precisely the wrong thing. He was a scrappy guy. He was not going to let a couple of punks rip him off. And he almost lost his life. The first rule if you are robbed is, *Don't resist*. And don't try to outsmart your assailant. You may be tempted to distract or delay the robber. Or you may feign an illness and pretend to collapse. You may fumble about, muttering that you can't find your wallet or that your ring won't come off. Such tactics might work. You might delay the robber long enough to have someone come to your aid. But such action is highly risky. A robber is not a patient sort. He may be edgy, strung-out on drugs, or just plain vicious. Your delaying tactics may well provoke him to use his weapon. Is anything that you are carrying worth that?

Certainly don't try to be clever, or play amateur psychologist or try to appeal to the criminal's sympathy. If he were a sympathetic human being, he would be in another line of work. And don't try to make the criminal feel guilty. Don't say, "I've got a wife and family," or, "I'm old and sick." Such remarks are likely to inflame the psychopathic mentality. Don't get belligerent in word or deed. One woman told a robber, "I'll never forget your face." He promptly shot her in the head.

Take the experts' advice. What do criminals do when they themselves become crime victims? They do as they are told, with no questions asked. They know the risks of doing otherwise.

Do exactly what your assailant says, as quickly and with as few words as possible. Police files are filled with the injuries done to would-be heroes or victims who tried to outsmart hoodlums.

When you are confronted by an armed robber, you are in a no-win situation. The best that you can hope to do is cut your losses. You will lose something, money or valuables. But keep the loss down to that. When the thief offers you those ancient alternatives, "Your money or your life," make an intelligent choice.

If You Are Attacked

All the cooperation in the world is not going to help if you run into a thug with a sadistic streak. You may be assaulted even if you obey completely. Try to escape. Do so screaming at the top of your lungs. If you cannot get away, do whatever you can to protect yourself—bite, scratch, kick—and keep up the hollering.

Identification of Robbers

There is one helpful thing that you can do while being robbed. Mentally note every detail. You may be half-paralyzed with fear, but try to absorb everything you can. Notice how many people are involved in the robbery. What sex are they? How old? Hair color? Try to observe distinctive features such as scars, birthmarks, tattoos, or physical deformities. Does the culprits' appearance give you ethnic clues? What are they wearing? What are their weapons? Take note of their voices and any names used. If a car is involved, try to note the color, year, make, body, antenna, and license plate number. Above all, look for unique features that lift your description above generalities.

And report your robbery. Report everything that you can remember about it to the police. You may be so frightened after an assault that all you want to do is flee to the refuge and safety of your home. You may feel that there is nothing the police can do to stop street crime and even less likelihood that they will recover what you have lost. You may, in short, become one of the roughly 40 percent of all victims who fail to report robberies. But remember the old highway safety slogan, "The life you save may be your own." The criminal you help to put behind bars won't be around to plague you, your family, or your neighbors. Your cooperation is essential if the police are to apprehend criminals. Some crimes *are* solved. Street criminals tend to be habitual offenders. They are well known to the police. If you can give the police a good description of your assailant or assailants and the conditions of the robbery, they have at least a fighting chance of making an arrest. If you say nothing, they can achieve nothing.

Also, the police determine where and when to assign patrols in part on the frequency of crimes committed. So your crime report has practical value.

Robbery in the House

Not all robberies take place on the street. You can also be robbed in your home, though it is less common. Or you may stumble onto a burglar in your home, and burglary escalates into robbery. You learned in chapter 1 what you can do to reduce the chances of burglary. You can act in still other ways to avoid being robbed in your home.

Rule Number One is, *Never open your door to a stranger.* If the caller claims to be a salesperson, you can always say you are busy. Even if someone comes to your door in some sort of official-looking uniform, ask to see his or her credentials. If someone claims to have a telegram or other message for you, have the person slip it under the door. If someone comes to your door asking to use the phone, tell him or her to give you the number and message and say that you will make the call for the person. If the caller becomes at all threatening, call the police immediately.

Assume that you have made a mistake and have opened your door to a stranger who does turn out to be a robber. Or, the robber may have gotten inside by force. At this point, the rules are pretty much the same as when you are robbed on the street. And again, Rule Number One is, *Don't resist.* Do as you are told. If the robber says to lie down on the floor, do it. If he or she demands to know where your money or valuables are kept, show the intruder enough to placate him or her. Your objective is to get the criminal out of your house and to get yourself out of this fix safe and sound. Afterward, report to the police every detail of the crime that you can remember.

Robbery in Your Car

Always lock your car wherever you park it. Robbers have been known to hide in the backseats of cars, particularly in parking lots, waiting for the owners to return. Always have your keys ready when approaching your locked car. It is wise to look inside the car to make sure no one is in it before you enter. Once you get into the car, you are essentially trapped.

You should always drive, to the extent possible, on well-traveled, well-lighted streets. Keep your doors locked even while you are driving. When you stop, say at a traffic light, a robber may try to force his way into the backseat or passenger seat. If someone does try to get into your car, drive off, blowing the horn to attract attention. The noise may scare off the thief.

If the attempt to enter your car happens at an intersection, try to pull the car right. That maneuver will put you in the same direction as the traffic flow. Also, you will be turning into your assailant, which may have some defensive value.

Weapons and Warning Devices

Should you carry a gun on your person to protect yourself from robbery? Again, before carrying a weapon, ask yourself these questions: Is the weapon legal? Is the weapon safe to use?

Are you properly trained in using it? Do you know the limitations on the weapon? Do you know the law covering its use? You should be aware that the weapon may be wrested from you and used against you.

There are nonlethal weapons on the market today such as tear gas guns and Mace, which is supposed to render your attacker immobile. Before arming yourself with these nonlethal weapons, consult with your local police to find out both the legal limits on their availability and whether the police think carrying them is a good idea. Remember that Mace is like a gun—it can be used against you by your attacker.

The safest defensive item that you should carry is a whistle with a loud, piercing sound—a police-style whistle. But never wear a whistle on a chain around your neck. The robber may try to stop you from using the whistle by choking you with your own chain. Whistles are best carried in a purse, kept in a pocket, or worn around the wrist like a bracelet.

Even using the whistle requires a certain amount of discretion. You will have to size up the particular situation. The sound of the whistle may bring help—assuming someone hears it and understands what it means—hopefully the police. But suppose you find yourself in a robbery situation in an essentially deserted area. The robber may change his priority from getting your money to shutting you up first. And he could do it violently. Even so, carrying a whistle is advisable. Use it with judgment.

DON'TS AND DOS

Don't

- walk alone at night, particularly in unsafe neighborhoods.
- take shortcuts through deserted areas.
- let suspicious strangers engage you in conversation.
- carry more money than you can afford to lose.
- carry all your money in one place on your person.
- resist if robbed.
- carry a weapon.

Do

- find a companion to walk with whenever possible.
- keep to the middle of the sidewalk.
- walk briskly and with purpose.
- avoid suspicious-looking groups, particularly young males. Cross the street if necessary to avoid them.
- avoid occupied parked cars with the motors running.
- head for people, a lighted place, or a store if being followed.
- pay by check, credit card, or charge account to avoid carrying much cash.
- carry coins for emergency telephone calls.
- keep your car locked when parked *and* when driving.
- have your keys ready when approaching your locked car.
- check the front seat and backseat of your car before entering. Make sure no one is hiding in either.
- carry a whistle or another warning device.
- if attacked, try first to get away. Scream.
- pay close attention to details so you can describe your assailant or assailants.

Purse Snatching

It was practically a tradition. The first of every month, Sarah R.'s Social Security check arrived. Sarah would leave her apartment and walk down Columbus Avenue to the A & P. She bought a few things and cashed the check there. Afterward, if the weather was nice, Sarah stopped in the park, where the other ladies always gathered. And they would talk—about grandchildren, high prices, and neighborhood gossip. This routine was for Sarah one of the bright spots of the month.

On this day, Sarah had come out of the supermarket, clutching her purse firmly. She had also looped the strap over her wrist. One couldn't be too careful. It depressed her to think of how much the neighborhood had deteriorated in recent years.

Near an intersection, Sarah spotted young Mrs. Farber pushing her baby carriage. Mrs. Farber lived in her building. Sarah stopped. The baby was adorable. She bent over to chuck the baby's chin, talked to the mother briefly, and continued across the street. She was suddenly aware of pounding steps behind her. Sarah screamed as a young boy— he looked no more than thirteen—yanked at her purse strap. "Leggo!" he yelled. He yanked the strap so hard that it broke, and Sarah went sprawling to the ground.

The purse was recovered later in a trash receptacle several blocks away, the money gone. Sarah suffered a dislocated shoulder and bruises.

Sarah R. was the victim of a purse snatching. Statistically, purse snatchings and pocket pickings account for only 2 percent of all thefts reported to the police. The figures are misleading, however. According to the National Crime Survey, something like two-thirds of all purse-snatching victims do not report these crimes. Actually, purse snatching is rampant, particularly against older women. It is probably the most common street crime. The loss from a stolen purse can be substantial—particularly to someone like Sarah R., who counted heavily on a small, fixed income to live. In one recent survey, the average loss for a reported purse snatching was $129.

Some crimes are "opportunistic." Opportunism is common in purse snatching. But there is also an element of calculation. Both situations, opportunism and calculation, can be avoided.

Mistakes to Avoid

Sarah R.'s case offers almost an encyclopedia of mistakes. She suffered a serious financial loss because she had kept almost all of the money from her cashed Social Security check in her purse. She depended on that money for her survival. But it was not necessary for her to carry that check in the first place. She could easily have had the check deposited directly into a checking or savings account. The procedure is simple. Just ask your bank or savings and loan company to arrange it. Or you can arrange the deposit through your Social Security office. You can also have other retirement checks deposited directly to your account. Direct deposit costs you nothing.

A second mistake. Sarah R. had locked herself into a predictable routine. Every first of the month, she took her check to the same supermarket, by the same route, and at the same time. She cashed it and then went to chat with her friends in the park. Social Security recipients and mail carriers are not the only people who know when the checks arrive. Thieves know it too. And some of them are clever enough to note the predictable movements of people in a neighborhood—people like Sarah.

Next mistake. Sarah cashed her check and carried all of the money on her. Even though she did not use direct deposit, she still should have deposited most of the money in her bank. That way she could have cut her loss substantially when her purse was snatched.

As long as Sarah did carry her money with her, she should have put it in different places—some in the purse, some in a pocket, for example.

And Sarah went to the supermarket by herself. Purse snatchers prefer to accost someone who is alone. She should have tried to find a friend, a neighbor, or a grown son or daughter to walk with her, if at all possible. And, it would have helped for her occasionally to vary her route and time.

Sarah even made a mistake in the way that she carried her purse. The safest way is to carry a purse with the strap over one shoulder and the bag between your arm and body. If the purse has a clasp, keep the clasp side toward your body. If the strap is not long enough to hang from the shoulder, put your arm through the strap and hold the purse against your body. But do not loop the strap around the wrist the way that Sarah did. You may be risking a broken arm or a dislocated shoulder. The purse snatcher was determined to wrest that purse from her. And because of the way she held it, she ended up not only robbed but injured as well.

And while it is a hard habit for women to overcome, is carrying a purse *always* a necessity? Sarah, on this particular errand, might as easily have gotten by without her purse if she had put her money in a secure pocket.

We have said that the safest way to walk down a lightly traveled or dark street is down the middle of the sidewalk. But if it is daytime and the streets are relatively busy, you should do something a bit different to avoid purse snatchers. In this situation, carry the purse on the building side of the sidewalk and walk a little closer to the buildings. In that way, a prospective thief has less maneuverability to snatch your purse and run off.

When riding on public transportation, a bus or subway, the proper place for your purse is on your lap, with your hand firmly on it. Don't put it on an empty seat next to you. Don't put it on the floor. The safest seat on public transportation is nearest the driver or motorman. Avoid sitting too close to rear exits. The thief can seize the purse and be out the door before you know what has happened.

If you go into a restaurant or a cafeteria, never leave your purse on the table or the chair if you are going to be away—not for an instant. In the supermarket don't leave your purse in the shopping cart. You are sure to be distracted at some point. Keep your purse on your arm.

Public rest rooms are another place where you have to be careful about purses. Don't hang the purse on the hook on the door of the toilet stall. You are liable to see a hand come reaching over the top for it. Don't put it on the floor either. You are liable to see a hand come reaching under for it. And, most likely, you won't see these hands until it is too late. Keep the purse on your lap if possible.

Credit Cards and Identification

Imagine that, in spite of all your precautions, your purse is snatched. If it contains credit cards, phone the credit card companies and alert them not to honor these cards. For this purpose, keep a list at home of your credit cards and their numbers. This precaution can make reporting stolen cards much easier.

If your house keys are in your purse and there is also information in it disclosing your address, immediately contact a locksmith to have your locks rekeyed or changed. If you neglect to do so, you may find yourself a burglary victim as well as a purse-snatching victim.

And don't be one of the "silent majority" who fails to report a purse snatching. It is not likely that your money will be recovered. But when the police detect purse-snatching patterns in a neighborhood, they often beef up surveillance, and that means more protection for you next time.

DON'TS AND DOS

Don't

- carry more money in your purse than you can afford to lose.
- carry all your money in one place on your person.
- carry your purse on the side facing the street.
- loop your purse strap over your wrist.
- leave your purse unattended anywhere.

Do

- have Social Security and retirement checks mailed directly to your bank or electronically transferred.
- take someone with you on money errands like cashing a check.
- vary your routine when doing money errands.
- keep your purse on your lap with your hand firmly on it in public transportation.
- report stolen credit cards to the card companies.
- get new locks if your address and house keys were both in a stolen purse.
- report a purse snatching to the police.

Chain Snatching

In the summertime, especially in crowded cities, snatching of jewelry chains is all too common. Your only defense is not to wear chains outdoors during the warm months.

Pickpocketing

Leonard V. literally had his hands full. Once again he had made the mistake of putting off his Christmas shopping to the last minute. It was odd that it took him so long to get around to it. Actually, nothing pleased Leonard more than the look on his wife's face or his grandchildren's faces when they opened their gifts. The shopping plaza was jammed that morning. Leonard practically had to elbow his way through the crowd, since he held big packages in both arms. Then he saw her coming right at him—a young girl, pretty, wearing jeans and a pea jacket. She looked completely distracted, so distracted that she ran right into Leonard. He had a terrible time keeping his balance and juggling his parcels without dropping anything. But he couldn't really be mad. The girl had apologized with a dazzling smile. And she had even wished him a Merry Christmas.

It was not until Leonard unloaded his packages into his car that he realized his wallet was missing from his back pocket. He went back and reported the theft to the store security officer. Then it all fell into place—the crowd, the girl bumping into him, and the jostling behind him as he had tried to regain his balance.

Leonard V. had had his pocket picked, one of the most ancient of the thieves' arts. Leonard might have avoided the financial loss and aggravation had he known how pickpockets operate. Pickpockets like crowds—crowds in stores, theaters, restaurants, airline terminals, and railroad and bus stations. They like it where people are jammed together, bumping and brushing against one another. And they like teamwork, since they frequently operate in pairs.

The pretty young thing who bumped into Leonard was half of a pickpocket team. The jostling that Leonard had felt behind him was from her partner. When she and Leonard collided, Leonard's attention, understandably, was distracted. In that crowd, being bumped from behind seemed entirely natural. And because he was being jostled, Leonard never felt the hand that was filching his wallet.

Preventive Measures to Take

What could Leonard have done to prevent this theft? For one thing, he should not have carried his wallet in his back pocket. He should have carried it in an inside jacket pocket or in a front pocket of his trousers. Even buttoning the back pocket is not safe, since the pickpocket may simply slash the bottom of the pocket to get your wallet. Then you have lost your money *and* a pair of pants. Also, the jostling, instead of distracting Leonard, should have alerted him that he was being set up. Women can thwart pickpockets by using purses with an overhanging flap so that the purse is not open at the top. If the purse has a fastener, keep it fastened. If it has a zipper, zip it. It is much too easy for a skilled pickpocket to lift a wallet from an open purse.

Reporting the Theft

Report a stolen wallet immediately to store authorities. Frequently the thieves will take only the money or the money and credit cards. But they may dispose of the wallet, commonly in a trash receptacle in a rest room. Insist that the store officials make a search for the missing wallet. It is bad enough losing the money. But think of the added aggravation of losing your driver's license and other vital cards and papers carried in your wallet.

DON'TS AND DOS

Don't
- carry a wallet in your back pants pocket.
- carry a wallet in a purse that is opened at the top.

Do
- be suspicious in crowded places when people bump into you.
- report a picked pocket immediately to store security officials and the police.

Thefts from Your Car

Oliver and Laura C. had a small spat. Laura was annoyed that Oliver had parked so far in the rear of the parking lot. It would take them several minutes just to walk to the stores.

Oliver reminded Laura that a little exercise would not hurt her. The truth was that his own back was aching after all the shopping they had done that day. Between the backache and his annoyance at Laura, Oliver did not feel like transferring the packages to the trunk. Consequently, in the backseat was a new wide-head tennis racquet. Oliver was a serious player, ranked in the seniors' division at his club. Also, in back was an antique clock that they were to drop off later to have fixed.

Annoyed as he was, Oliver was not careless. He made sure all the windows were closed, and he locked the car as Laura walked off toward the shops.

When they returned twenty-five minutes later, the car's rear window had been smashed. The tennis racquet and antique clock were gone.

Thefts from cars occur even more commonly than purse snatchings or pocket pickings. Such thievery is made easy if people are careless. The thief does not even have to run the burglar's risk of entering a house or the robber's risk of actually confronting the victim.

Avoiding Mistakes

Oliver made it a little tougher for the thief by closing the car windows and locking the door, but he did not go far enough. Laura was right. He should not have parked on the outer edge of the parking lot. The closer in, the safer. The more likely that others can see someone tampering with your car, the better. That goes for choosing the street where you park your car too. Also, a robber is more likely to accost someone returning to a car in a remote part of a lot or street.

If you do have to leave packages in the car, leave them in the trunk. If you leave things inside the car, at least put them out of sight—in the glove compartment, if they will fit, or under a seat. Things left on a backseat, as Oliver discovered, stand out temptingly like goodies behind an untended candy counter.

It is distressing but true that items stolen from cars will probably not be recovered.

DON'TS AND DOS

Don't
- leave anything on the seats of your car.
- park in remote, unlit, unwatched places.

Do
- keep the car locked and the windows closed.
- stow parcels and valuables out of sight, preferably in a locked trunk.

3 Car Theft

Roy M. was a fussbudget about his car, a two-year-old maroon hardtop. Roy maintained the car, with twenty-two thousand miles on it, in showroom condition. Roy's wife, Anne, said that if he lavished half as much attention on her, she might look as good as the car. They had kidded each other like that throughout thirty-five years of marriage.

On this winter morning, Roy had taken Anne to the doctor to get her hypertension prescription renewed. He had found a parking place half a block from the doctor's office. Roy had told Anne that he would wait in the car.

He watched her make her way gingerly down the street. It was a blustery day, and the sidewalks were slick with ice.

Suddenly Roy's heart leaped. He saw Anne slip and come down hard on the pavement. He sprang from the car and ran to her as fast as he could. Passersby had already stopped to help her. She was wincing in pain. She said she thought she might have sprained her ankle. A passing letter carrier helped Roy bring Anne up to the doctor's office.

After the doctor brought Anne into the examining room, Roy took a seat in the waiting room. Suddenly he remembered something. He quickly took the elevator down to the street and started trotting up the block toward his car. It was gone.

The car was never recovered. The next month was particularly difficult for them, carless and with Anne on crutches while they waited for the insurance company to settle the claim on the stolen car. Roy had loved that car. And this was the only time that he ever remembered leaving the key in the ignition.

Roy M. had become a victim of a major business in the United states, the stolen-car industry. Over a million cars are stolen in this country every year—one approximately every thirty seconds. In a recent year, one out of every 158 registered motor vehicles was stolen. The car losses, police investigation costs, and other related expenses total over $5 billion per year.

Car thefts hurt the victim most, but, in the end, all drivers pay. Insurance claims for all those stolen cars mean higher premiums for all owners. The Illinois State's Attorney's Office offers vivid proof. As the Illinois driver moves from areas of low to high car theft, insurance premiums for the identical car skyrocket. Comprehensive coverage that costs $54 in one small downstate city rises to $450 for the same car in Chicago's loop area. Much of that increase is explained by higher auto thefts.

Car theft has changed substantially over the past twenty years, and for the worst. During the early 1960s, for example, most cars were taken by joyriders, kids who likely found the keys in a car and who decided to go for a spin. In those days, about 90 percent of all stolen cars were recovered. But, as time went on, car theft became more and more the game of professionals. Slick, quick thieves now steal cars for resale or for their salable parts. Selling parts has become highly lucrative. The demand for hoods, doors, and fenders is tremendous. Consequently, stolen cars are often taken to so-called chop shops, where within minutes crews wielding acetylene torches cut out the most valuable parts. A door on a big luxury car, for example, can be worth up to five hundred dollars. The front end even on an economy car may bring twenty-five hundred dollars. Cars offer one situation where the sum of the parts is equal to more than the whole.

Little wonder that today stolen cars are not easily found. Since the underworld took over the car-theft business, recoveries have fallen steeply. Where nine out of ten stolen cars were recovered in 1960, only 51.7 percent of them were recovered in 1982, the latest year for which figures are available and the year showing the lowest recovery rate in automotive history.

While car theft is high nationwide, you stand a greater chance of losing your car if you live in a big city. The nation's five major metropolitan areas—New York, Los Angeles, Chicago, Detroit, and Boston—account for almost a third of all car thefts.

An amazing number of cars are stolen because of carelessness. The keys are left in the ignition in about 40 percent of all stolen-car cases. And 80 percent of all stolen cars had been left unlocked. Then there are the truly hopeless cases who leave their cars running as they, for example, pop in somewhere to buy a pack of cigarettes.

The first defense against car theft is to take the keys out of the ignition, roll up the windows, and lock the doors.

Even then, is your car completely safe? Not against the skilled car thief. Watch this pro in action. He or she scouts residential areas or parking lots late at night. That's where and when two-thirds of all auto thefts take place. The thief may even be stealing a car "on order"—by make, year, and model—for a crooked dealer. The car racket is that well organized. Our thief finds the desired car on a quiet street. The car is locked. The windows are closed. No problem. The thief takes out a tool called a slim-jim and slides it between the window and the door, then easily unlocks the door. He or she also has various tools in a kit to break the ignition lock or pull the lock out. An adept thief can break into a locked car and be off in under sixty seconds. Even the legal risks are not all that high. Fewer than 14 percent of auto thefts result in the arrest of the thief.

Another lucrative market for thieves, besides spare parts, is the overseas sale of stolen cars. Americans may be importing Hondas and Toyotas by the boatload, but the big American sedan is still a hot item in Latin America and Middle Eastern countries. Roy M.'s maroon hardtop may be cruising down Mexico City's Paseo de la Reforma by now.

Preventive Measures to Take

Since car thieves are so adept, what can a driver do to stop them? Lock your car at all times. Eight out of ten cars stolen were left unlocked. Also, park only on or in well-lighted, busy streets or parking lots. Park with your front wheels turned sharply to the right or left. That makes it harder for a thief to tow the car away.

Many people like to put a spare car key in a little magnetic box and hide it on their car. That way, if they lose their keys, or lock them in the car, they can still get in. That way the thief can also steal your car. The thief will figure out your hiding place through the same reasoning that you did. So don't hide a spare key on your car.

There are other precautions you can take as well. Every vehicle has its own Vehicle Identification Number, its VIN. The VIN is stamped into the metal on the vehicle's engine or transmission. The VIN looks something like this: IF 23FIL236093. The VIN is the best lead that the police have in tracking a stolen vehicle.

That being the case, thieves will try to remove the VIN and replace it with another number. They may buy an identical wrecked model and switch the VIN from the wreck to the stolen car.

Therefore, it's a good idea for you to repeat your car's VIN somewhere else on your car where it won't be spotted easily. You might use an electric etching tool for this purpose. You might also slip a piece of paper with your name and address on it, or a business card, into the car door interior.

Antitheft Devices

As with the burglar, it is tough to stop a determined car thief. Still, car thieves, like burglars, are looking for the easiest mark. There are a number of antitheft car devices that you can buy to make his job harder. None are theft-proof. But they may deter a thief just enough to pass your car by.

For instance, you can buy an alarm that goes off when someone tries to break into your car. Some alarms will even go off if one end of your car is lifted by someone trying to tow it away. Vehicle alarms are not cheap. They start at about $150. But considering what your car cost, their protection can be a bargain.

A less expensive protection is a fuel cutoff. This device costs about $65, installed. The fuel cutoff allows the car to run only until the fuel in the carburetor or fuel line is used up. After about a block, the car stops.

Or, you might buy a heavy-duty ignition lock for about $125. This lock prevents the thief from yanking out your ignition. But the pro can still cut through the plastic or soft metal encasing your steering column in order to bypass the ignition.

You may be able to defray part of the cost of these safety items. Many auto insurance companies will give discounts to drivers who install antitheft devices on their cars.

Some police departments will etch all the car windows with the VIN and will place Vehicle Identification Program decals on both front door windows, thus reducing the automobile's value to any chop shop. Check with your local police department. This service is also available through some car dealers.

No device is perfect. Prevention is a game of wits with your trying to slow the thief down while the thief tries to penetrate your defenses.

Theft of a car is a financial loss and an inconvenience. The risks cannot be completely eliminated, but they can be reduced.

DON'TS AND DOS

Don't

- leave your car key in the ignition.
- park in dark, isolated streets or parking lots.
- leave the registration or title anywhere in the car.
- hide a spare key on the car.

Do

- lock your doors and roll up the windows at all times.
- park with your front wheels turned sharply to one side to hinder illicit towing.
- etch your Vehicle Identification Number in an obscure place on your car.
- consider installing the most effective antitheft car device that you can afford.

4 Con Artists and Swindles

The Pigeon Drop

Edna P., seventy-two, had taken a seat on a park bench, enjoying the sun and watching the people pass by. As she sat there, a young woman carrying a shopping bag stopped and said to Edna, "Do you mind if I sit here for a few minutes and take a load off my feet?"

Edna smiled and moved aside to make room for her. The young woman struck up a conversation, and Edna found her "sweet and friendly." She was especially impressed by the young woman's cheerful attitude—especially since, Edna learned in the course of their conversation, she had recently been widowed. The woman's husband had died in an automobile accident, leaving her with a small child to raise alone. Edna instinctively liked her.

They had been talking for about ten minutes when a young man came by and stopped in front of the park bench. He glanced under the bench with a puzzled expression and said to Edna, "Did you drop this, ma'am?" He bent down to pick up a paper bag from under the bench. "It's not mine," Edna answered. She then looked to the young woman, who shook her head and said, "It's not mine, either."

The young man opened the bag, saying, "Maybe

52

there's some identification in it." As he did, his eyes popped. "Wow! Look at this!" He held the bag open so Edna could see.

The bag appeared to be full of money, neatly wrapped packages of twenty-dollar bills. The young woman peered inside and gasped. "What should we do with it?" she said. Edna, who had never seen so much money in her life, looked to the young man.

"My father's a police lieutenant," he said. "Let me call him and find out." He handed the bag with the money in it to the young woman and asked her to hold it while he went to a nearby phone booth.

Edna was excited. There were few adventures in her life these days. She was glad the young man had proved so honest, but on the other hand, the sight of all that money had set her pulse racing.

The young man came back and said, "My father claims under the law that it's 'Finders, keepers' as long as nobody claims the money in a week."

A thought went through Edna's mind. Who were the "finders" in this case? The young man went on, "And I guess in all fairness, all three of us really found it." Edna felt relieved.

"All we have to do, my dad says," the young man continued, "is turn the money in at the police station. If nobody claims it after a week, it's ours to split three ways. But we have to put up a five-hundred-dollar good faith bond."

The young man seemed to sense the uneasiness in Edna's eyes. "Dad says he'll take personal responsibility for the money and the bond. Here, let me write down his name and number at the station house." He wrote something on a slip of paper and started to hand it to the young woman.

She shook her head. "I certainly can't put up the bond money," she said. Then she gave the slip of paper to Edna. It read, "Lt. George Brannigan," followed by the police department phone number.

There was an awkward pause. "I guess we'll just have to turn in the money and forget about splitting it," the young man said.

Edna stared at the slip of paper and sighed. "I suppose I could go to the bank," she said.

The young man and woman accompanied Edna to her house to get her bankbook. On the way over, the young fellow said confidentially, "Dad mentioned we shouldn't tell a soul about this. Money in a bag like that is probably stolen, and if the thieves catch on, we've had it." He made a throat-cutting gesture with his hand. Edna felt a shiver of fear.

Later, outside the bank, Edna handed five hundred dollars to the young man, who said he would take it and the bag of money directly to his father at the police station. Before he left, he reminded Edna and the young woman again about maintaining total secrecy.

Edna waited impatiently for the week to pass. Then she hurried to the police station to see Lieutenant Brannigan, praying that no one had claimed the money.

No one had claimed it because there was no money. There was no Lieutenant Brannigan. And there was no five-hundred-dollar "bond" left. The police sat the stunned woman down and explained that she had been swindled. The young woman who sat next to her on the park bench was the "catch girl." She had planted the bag with the money under the park bench when Edna wasn't watching. The twenty-dollar bills were only the top of each package. The rest was newspaper cut to bill size. The young man who "found" the bag was her accomplice, the "hit man."

Edna P. was the victim of a classic swindle, the "pigeon drop." *Pigeon* is the con artist's word for "a sucker."

Most older Americans fear becoming the victims of violent crime. Yet, far more older people are the victims of reported economic crimes such as the pigeon drop than of violent crimes. The President's Commission on Law Enforcement and the Administration of Justice reported that twice as many dollars are lost through fraud than through robbery, burglary, larceny, and auto theft combined.

Older persons, especially people living alone, are prime targets for con artists. Often they are lonely and feel isolated from the mainstream of life. They want human contact and innocently welcome the swindler's friendly advances.

Older women are particularly vulnerable. Mary Carey and George Sherman in a book entitled *A Compendium of Bunk or How to Spot a Con Artist* (Springfield, Ill.: Charles C Thomas, Publisher, 1976), write as follows:

> Elderly women in somewhat reduced circumstances are the ones who do have money—real money—in the bank. They are not paying off debts incurred for new furniture or new cars. They usually have some small inheritance from a deceased spouse. They are fearful of illness and they are fearful of being a burden on their children. They want a little something put by, and they will scrimp and save to get it. They need the security.
>
> And, after years of scrimping and saving and planning and budgeting, they can be intoxicated at the thought of a sudden windfall. If they possess even the tiniest iota of greed, it can be excited so that they forget, for the moment, the habits of a lifetime.

According to research carried out in the state of California, 90 percent of pigeon drop victims are older citizens, with the average victim being seventy. In that state alone, people are swindled out of nearly a half-million dollars a year by this scheme. The police believe that for every case reported, five more are not. Consequently, most con artists are not caught and are free to go on carrying out their vicious deceptions. The Los Angeles Police Department reported that during one six-month span, older persons lost more money through the pigeon drop than banks did through robberies.

Commander John Murphy of the New York City police, an expert on frauds and con games, testified before a congressional committee in 1976 about twenty-five typical swindles in his files. Of the twenty-five victims, fifteen were aged fifty-five or older. Their average loss was $5,933. Losses of the younger victims were far lower, an average of $770.

"When the younger people get taken," Commander Murphy said, "they lose a few hundred, a thousand, sometimes four or five, but the older people will give up just about every cent they have in the bank. They get wiped out."

The commander went on to give a graphic portrait of the tragedy that swindles cause among older victims:

If you want to see a horror story, when we get a victim down at the office, a victim in her seventies, she comes in and she will sit there. First of all, she has tremendous shame that she was conned. It is almost like a crime of rape. She will sit down and start telling the story, and she is embarrassed and shaken. When you realize [these people] just lost their life savings or that crutch that helps them stave off poverty, when you see the realization hitting them that they are going to have to move, [or that] they have nothing to leave their grandchildren—things like that— you can see a dead person in front of you, as brutal as it sounds.

We had a woman last week who lost like thirty-three thousand dollars. That is a lot of money, but she is not a wealthy woman. [It was] her life savings [from] insurance payments when her husband died. She sat there and we had to shake her by the shoulders to question her. She stared into nothing. I asked her if she had somebody to go home to at night, somebody we could call. I was afraid that this poor woman was going out of a window. She did not, but I was afraid she would get sick. I think they die more quickly when they've lost their pride.

Losing all their money is bad enough. For some older people, Commander Murphy testified, there is more to it than money:

Once the victim loses her savings, she is very embarrassed and ashamed to come forward. Also, at her age, she worries that possibly her family will think that she is becoming senile and cannot make it on her own and cannot take care of herself. A lot of women feel that way, and it affects them that way also. They are afraid their families are going to find out what has happened.

The con artist is essentially a crooked actor and often a highly skilled one. The expression *con artist* is derived from the word *confidence*. Confidence lies at the heart of these criminals' successes. The criminals succeed because they are able to win over people's confidence. Don't expect a con artist to be someone who looks like a crook—someone shifty-eyed, tough-talking, and dressed like a thug. Con artists try to look like anybody else who is honest and respectable. They are usually neatly and conventionally dressed. The men may wear coats and ties; the women may wear dresses. They are courteous, sympathetic, often likable people, and they are good listeners. They are clever street psychologists too. They understand human behavior and emotions. Above all, they know how to manipulate those emotions.

Con artists do not pick their victims haphazardly. They are careful to locate persons with financial resources—persons whose confidence they can win, persons who are emotionally vulnerable and whom they can manipulate.

Here, typically, is how these charlatans go about finding victims. A local newspaper is one starting point. The paper may carry a story about someone in your town receiving a large insurance settlement, winning a cash prize, or coming into an inheritance. The con artist now has the name of someone known to have money and a way to introduce himself or herself into that person's life: "Say, aren't you the Mrs. Green who . . ."

To shrewd con artists, the telephone book is also a useful tool. If they are looking for older people, biblical first names offer a good clue: Josiah, Ruth, Rebecca. If the telephone is listed under "Rebecca Robinson," there's a fair chance that they have located a woman living alone.

You may be the sort of good citizen who donates money to worthy causes. Con artists are resourceful enough to obtain lists of such contributors. They also find out in this way which charities interest you and that you are a person who may listen to a heartwarming appeal for that cause.

Or the con artist may case your neighborhood, noticing who lives where, what banks people use, and who appears to live alone. They are often open and friendly and will strike up conversations to learn more about you and your neighbors.

Once a promising target has been picked, the next step is for the con artist to win over the potential victim's confidence. How do these swindlers go about convincing a normally intelligent person to hand over money to a total stranger? Trust is the key. And here is how the con artist goes about winning your trust. First of all, he or she will likely not arouse suspicion by manner or dress. Con artists are usually polite, well spoken, and friendly. The well-briefed con artist will hit all the right trust buttons. The swindler may say that he or she was referred to you by your minister, priest, or rabbi or that he or she talked to this friend or that relative of yours. These familiar and trusted names may allay your fears, though the swindler has probably never laid eyes on any of these people.

The clever con artist will probably offer his or her credentials even before you think to ask about them—business cards or letters of recommendation. He or she may even wear an official-looking uniform and look like a police officer or fire fighter, complete with an impressive badge.

Con artists know in advance what is likely to trouble you about their scheme, and they will have good answers ready. The talented swindlers not only have a knack for making you trust them, but they are also such good amateur psychologists that they make you feel guilty if you *do not* trust them.

Having won your trust, the next tactic of the con artist is to manipulate your emotions. And one of the surefire emotions is the potential victim's greed—the desire to get something for nothing, to bet on a sure thing, to reap a windfall, to make a killing.

Finally, the con artist has to sell you on secrecy to make a scheme work. Naturally, if you check out the deal with legitimate authorities, or even a clearheaded friend or relative, the scheme is going to fall through. Not only that, but if the person you check with is a law-enforcement official, the con artist is in serious trouble. He or she has to persuade you to tell no one about this fantastic opportunity. And the reason you have to keep it a secret will always make a certain sense.

Another tip-off that you are dealing with a crook is the con artist's insistence on speed. It's always, "We have to do this right away, before the banks close," or "before the offer expires," or "before 'someone' has to leave town." If you have time to talk to someone or to change your mind, the con artist knows he or she is sunk. So the pressure is always on you to move quickly.

Thus the con artist follows a predictable pattern: find a promising victim, win over the victim's confidence, manipulate the victim's emotions, insist on secrecy, and move quickly. Edna P.'s case was a perfect example. She had been scouted in advance by the hit team. They knew that she lived alone. They knew that she had money and in which bank. They knew her habits, such as sitting in the park.

The pigeon drop can be worked in several different ways. In another version, the hit man comes by and spots the bag of money. But this time, he may offer to telephone his lawyer for advice. Or he says he is going to call his friend, who is a vice-president at the bank. From there on it's pretty much the same. The money has to be held for a certain period before it belongs to the finders, and the pigeon is expected to put up a "good faith" bond or deposit. That is the last the victim ever sees of the con artist. Notice that in each of these variations, the advice always comes from persons of authority—police officers, lawyers, or bankers. This use of impressive and trustworthy figures is one way that the con artist dispels your doubts. You will see this psychological trick used again and again in the frauds that are described in the following pages.

The pigeon drop is probably the most frequent scam worked against older people. One police fraud expert estimates that there are as many as eight hundred different swindles. But, he sadly concludes, "Who needs new con games when the old ones like the pigeon drop keep on working so successfully?" Wouldn't it be marvelous if just once, when the "pigeon" is asked, "Did you drop this bag?" he or she would say, "Why, yes, I did," and just walk off with it?

The Bank Examiner

Ernest Q., sixty-seven, lived alone in an apartment in an Ohio city. He was a quiet man, well liked by his neighbors and active in church and civic affairs. Early on a Friday afternoon, Ernest received a telephone call. The caller identified himself as a "Mr. Martin, an investigator with the district office of the Federal Reserve System." Mr. Martin asked Ernest if he still maintained an account at a certain bank. Ernest answered that he did. Mr. Martin explained that there were some problems at the bank, but Ernest was not to be alarmed. The trouble could be worked out if depositors cooperated. Ernest *was* alarmed. Most of what he had in this world was in that bank account. Mr. Martin then asked if he might come to Ernest's apartment to explain the situation confidentially and to tell him what needed to be done to protect the depositors.

Ernest readily agreed to the appointment. The last thing Mr.· Martin told Ernest was that he should not mention their conversation to anyone in order to protect the security of the investigation.

Within an hour, Mr. Martin—a distinguished silver-haired man in a gray three-piece suit, with the manner of quiet authority—was at Ernest's door. He introduced himself and drew a billfold from his breast pocket. He flipped it open, revealing a laminated ID card and a heavy silver shield.

Ernest asked Mr. Martin to come in and sit down. Martin did, asking Ernest if he had discussed the matter with anyone. Ernest answered no. Martin then asked, "How long have you done business with the bank?"

"For over fifteen years," Ernest answered anxiously. "Please, tell me, what's going on?"

The man opened his attaché case, took out several bank ledgers, and glanced at them. "You have a sizable account, don't you?" He looked directly at Ernest.

Ernest hesitated for a moment, then nodded.

"Here's the problem," Martin explained. "When we audited the bank a few weeks ago, we turned up irregularities. We're pretty sure that one of the assistant managers is embezzling. He's worked out a way of falsifying the records of deposits and withdrawals. He usually pulls his scheme on older customers depositing or withdrawing substantial sums." Martin looked Ernest right in the eye. "We asked the bank officials to recommend two or three of their best customers—good citizens, the kind of person the government could trust—to get to the bottom of this business. You were their first recommendation."

Ernest smiled shyly.

"Here's what we're asking you to do," Martin went on. "We'd like you to go to the bank this afternoon and make a fairly large withdrawal. But don't draw out everything—just about 90 percent of your account."

Ernest looked at the man skeptically. Martin did not appear to notice. He continued without interruption.

"The lifetime savings of hundreds of innocent people like yourself are at stake. We know you're a civic-minded man. We hope you will cooperate. After you make the withdrawal, my staff will have a bonded messenger sent here. He'll give you a receipt for the money and return to my office to make photographs of it and to record the serial numbers. That's how we're going to catch the embezzler." He looked again at Ernest. "A lot of people will be counting on you. Will you help?"

Ernest hesitated, then nodded.

Martin then asked if he could use his phone to call Ernest's bank. Ernest agreed. He heard Martin say, "Yes. He's going to help us. Like you said, he's a fine man. Yes. I'm arranging for a bonded messenger to take in his withdrawal to the Federal Reserve office."

Mr. Martin then drove Ernest to the bank, waited outside for him, and then drove him back home. Ernest had drawn out eighteen thousand dollars in cash.

They had been back at his apartment only a few minutes when a uniformed man, introduced as the bonded messenger, arrived at the door. He carefully counted the money and gave Ernest a receipt. After the messenger left, Mr. Martin stayed for a few more minutes. He stressed the absolute secrecy required until the embezzler could be arrested. Ernest was not to tell a soul what had happened. Martin said that he would call Ernest after the arrest on Monday morning. At that time, Ernest could come to the district office to reclaim his money.

That Monday morning, Ernest waited nervously for the call. When two o'clock came and he still had heard nothing, he tried to call the district office of the Federal Reserve system himself. There was no such listing. In desperation he next called the bank manager and heard the chilling words, "I'm afraid, sir, you've been swindled."

Ernest Q. was the victim of another classic con game, the "bank examiner" scheme. Again, Ernest was not a casual choice. The con artists had scouted him carefully. They had learned about his civic activities. They had found out where he did his banking.

They had dispelled his doubts by appearing legitimate. "Mr. Martin" looked right. He spoke right. He had credentials. There was the call to Ernest's bank and the bonded messenger in uniform. Also, the con man worked on Ernest's self-esteem. Ernest felt that he had to cooperate as a duty to other depositors like himself.

You may find it inconceivable that anyone would hand over so large a sum of money to a perfect stranger. But bank officials and law-enforcement people tell us that the bank examiner scheme is pulled off all the time, and with heartbreaking consequences.

Like the pigeon drop, the bank examiner scheme is worked several different ways. If you are approached by someone claiming to be a bank examiner, a police officer, or a bank official who wants your help in uncovering a bank irregularity, be on your guard. Call someone you know and trust at the bank. Or call the police. Under no circumstances reveal your account number or bank balance to strangers, no matter how "official" they may appear. Above all, never draw a dime from your bank and give it to such a person.

The Home Inspector

Arthur N. lived with his bedridden sister in an old residential neighborhood of Boston. Arthur answered his door one winter afternoon to a man who identified himself as a "city safety inspector." He showed Arthur his identification card, which he wore clipped to his jacket. He had come to inspect the house's wiring and heating systems, he said. Arthur was puzzled. He had never heard of this inspection before. And he and his sister had lived in the house for over fifty years.

The inspector saw Arthur's confusion. "It's a new city ordinance just passed last year. You mean you never heard about it?"

Arthur felt embarrassed and said, "Oh, I guess I read something about it in the *Herald*."

The inspector then asked Arthur to show him to the cellar. Arthur led the way. Then he heard his sister calling from upstairs wanting to know what was happening. He went up to explain.

Fifteen minutes later, the inspector came back with a grim expression on his face. He told Arthur that the electrical system checked out okay. But the burner in the furnace was faulty. It had to be replaced immediately. Otherwise, the inspector could not certify the furnace for further use. "How fast could your sister get out of the house?" the inspector asked ominously. "That burner could go any minute."

Arthur panicked. It was late in the day. The weather was bitterly cold. How, he wondered, was he going to get somebody to fix the furnace on such short notice?

The inspector turned out to be understanding. "Look, I know you're in a jam. Let me see what I can do. I've got a buddy. He's retired like you. He used to fix furnaces for . . ." He mentioned the name of a well-known local plumbing and heating contractor. "I could give him a call. Maybe he'd come over and do it."

Arthur looked hopeful.

The man asked to use Arthur's phone to call his friend. After the call, he said, "He can come over this afternoon. The job will cost $350, parts and labor. He has to be paid cash because he doesn't want anything fouling up his Social Security. Actually," the inspector went on, "it's a bargain. This guy's got no overhead, and he doesn't charge union scale. What do you say?"

Arthur was depressed by the unexpected expense, but, thinking of his sister upstairs and the frigid temperature outside, he saw no choice but to accept.

"I'll give you a call in the morning," the inspector said. "If the work is done, I'll come back and certify the furnace." He started to go. As he was leaving, the inspector added, "By the way, the county says we're not supposed to recommend service people. If anybody found out I'd fixed you up, I'd lose my job." He winked. "So keep it to yourself, okay?"

Arthur agreed. Not long afterward the repairman arrived, finished the job, and was paid in cash.

Of course, there was nothing wrong with Arthur's furnace. The "inspector" was a phony. Furthermore, the new burner installed was put in wrong, requiring more work and expense by a legitimate repairman.

Arthur had been bilked by another longtime scheme, the "furnace inspector" swindle. He was not alone. Con artists working this dodge look for neighborhoods like Arthur's, where the homes are old and the residents tend to be older persons. Arthur was one of a half-dozen people conned by the furnace scheme in his neighborhood that day.

The classic elements of the swindle are present here: a carefully targeted victim, the winning of confidence (again by the appearance of authority), the manipulation of emotion (this time fear), the need for secrecy, and the pressure to act fast. Con artists always follow this formula.

Here are some variations on the furnace inspector swindle. Your tree is so decayed that unless it is cut down it will fall on your home. Your hot-water heater is about to blow up and must be replaced immediately. Your electrical wiring is so bad that, unless something is done right now, your house will burn down.

Home-Repair Frauds

In the typical home-repair fraud, workmen "just happen to be in your neighborhood" and notice a hole in your roof, a broken gutter, a sag in your house's foundation, or crumbling blacktop in the driveway. They offer a bargain price if you will let them do the job right away. They have some leftover material—blacktop, paint, drainpipe—with them. You are only going to be charged for labor. The emotion appealed to here is our love of a bargain. Almost all home-repair frauds are variations on this theme. The victim's complaints are enough to make a statue weep: paint that washes off with the first rain, aluminum siding that peels as the repairman drives off into the sunset, lightning conductors made of painted rope. A scriptwriter could not think of the preposterous frauds that are practiced every day upon the public.

The Hearing-Aid Scam

In the hearing-aid scam, a salesperson arrives at your door asking to demonstrate a new model hearing aid. You explain that there is nothing wrong with your hearing. The salesperson goes on to say that that's not really important. You really don't have to buy anything. The salesperson is working his or her way through college and gets paid ten dollars for every demonstration, whether you buy or not. You aren't obliged to do anything except observe the demonstration, which will only take a few minutes.

Afterward, the salesperson asks you to sign a form and says, "This is to prove to my boss that I actually demonstrated the hearing aid for you." It turns out that what you signed was a contract to buy a hearing aid for perhaps $250. You have been hoodwinked.

Salting the Mine

Back in the gold rush days, the con artist of yesteryear would scatter some real gold nuggets around a worked-out or useless mine. He could then convince a prospective buyer that he was buying into a rich vein. The gullible prospector wound up getting no gold, only the shaft.

This form of swindle is known as "salting the mine." And it is still used down to the present day. In one West Coast city, a con artist bought a half-dozen television sets from a retailer at the full price. He then sold them for one-fifth of what he paid. He next hired people to work as telephone solicitors offering "carloads" of TV sets to be sold at distress discounts by a bankrupt retail chain. To prove his claim, prospective buyers were told about the six satisfied customers whom they could call. The buyers were then informed that they had to pay cash in advance (the old hurry-up tactic) and delivery would be in two weeks.

No television sets were delivered, of course. But the con artist raked in nearly sixty thousand dollars before the police learned about his scheme. He had won over his customers' confidence by "salting the mine."

The crimes that get the most attention are those that arouse the most fear: burglary, rape, robbery, and murder. People rarely hear about frauds; consequently, they are not alert to them. However, scams—particularly those perpetrated against older people living on fixed incomes, pensions, and Social Security—cause their own kind of cruelty. Be aware of them.

DON'TS AND DOS

Don't

- give personal information, particularly financial information, about yourself to strangers.
- advertise that you live alone by the way you list your name in the phone book or put it on your mailbox.
- be fooled by a trustworthy manner or by an official-sounding position of any person who makes an unusual financial proposition to you. Check the person out first.
- be fooled by credentials, badges, or uniforms.
- give a stranger money or valuables, as a "good faith" deposit or "proof of trust."
- be taken in by offers too good to be true. They usually aren't good and aren't true.
- sign anything that you don't understand.
- be pressured to act quickly on any business proposal.

Do

- be suspicious of "officials" supposedly calling from government agencies, banks, or the police. Check them out.
- be wary of strangers with money propositions claiming to have been referred by your friends, relatives, or clergy.
- be instantly suspicious of "deals" that require secrecy.
- be immediately suspicious of "deals" requiring that you act immediately.
- take a few days to consider money propositions.
- consult with someone you trust if asked to turn over money. Call a friend, lawyer, or banker.
- report to the police if victimized. Don't let your pride allow a con artist to go unpunished.

5 *Medical Charlatans*

Grace and Gladys B., sisters both in their sixties, lived together in a small town in the South. Until recently, Grace had worked as a bookkeeper for a soft drink distributor. But when Gladys became ill, Grace left her job and stayed home to look after her sister.

At first, Gladys's ailment proved puzzling and difficult to diagnose. Eventually Gladys was found to be suffering from cancer of the lymph system, lymphosarcoma. Naturally, this diagnosis had an upsetting effect on Grace as well as on Gladys. The sisters were inseparable.

Their family physician referred Gladys to a specialist, and the specialist counseled radiation and surgery.

Gladys was familiar with the difficult side effects of radiation, and the thought of surgery terrified her. She begged Grace not to put her in the hospital. Thus, immediate medical treatment was delayed.

Then one day Grace came home from grocery shopping full of hope. She had run into a former co-worker, who told Grace about an extraordinary cancer treatment. It did not require surgery or radiation. It was called the immunology treatment. The patient need only take certain injections that would stimulate the body's immune system to destroy the cancer. The woman said that a cousin of hers had a neighbor who had been cured through this treatment.

Unfortunately, the immunology treatment was not available from physicians in their area. As Grace's friend explained it, cancer was "big business" for doctors. And they were not about to endorse a relatively simple, natural cure. Doing so could cost them income.

Gladys was delighted when Grace gave her the news. She pleaded with her sister to look further into the new treatment. Grace did. But no matter what doctors she asked, she got the same answer. The immunology treatment was useless and even dangerous if it delayed people from getting legitimate cancer therapy. Grace started to believe what her friend had told her about doctors.

Then one evening the sisters received a call from a Doctor B. He claimed to be a pioneer in cancer immunology therapy, and he said that someone had told him of Grace's inquiries on behalf of Gladys. The two sisters were instantly interested. Unfortunately, because of the resistance of the American medical establishment, Doctor B. said that he had to treat patients outside of the country at his clinic in the Bahamas. He offered to arrange Gladys's admission to the clinic and for Grace to stay with her.

Dr. B.'s call seemed to the two sisters like a reprieve from hell. They virtually exhausted their savings to make the trip and to enter Gladys in the clinic in the Bahamas. Grace stayed nearby in a hotel. There was a point in the first few weeks of the immunology treatment when Gladys actually began to feel better. Her ever-present pain lessened. She felt more energetic. Her appetite picked up. But then she began to fail, though faithful to the immunology regimen.

Within two months, Gladys B. was dead. The form of cancer that she died from, under proper care, is considered treatable and has a good survival rate. But precious time had been lost in the immunology treatment.

One can feel nothing but the deepest sympathy and compassion for people like Grace and Gladys. They were driven by desperation on the one hand and hope on the other. These two emotions are the most effective weapons of the medical quack. And the fraud that quacks practice is heartless and cruel.

Older Americans need to be especially alert to phony medical personnel and practices. Illness is sometimes a companion of the aging process. For the older patient with a difficult-to-treat or terminal illness, the willingness to try anything is not surprising. When people become desperate enough, they are likely to feel that they have nothing to lose. The quack knows this. Consequently, according to the House Select Committee on Aging, 60 percent of all medical quackery is aimed at older patients.

The quack, it seems, has always been with us. Archaeologists have unearthed a hair restorer that an ancient Egyptian queen tried on her son's bald head over five thousand years ago. It was made of the hoof of an ass, the wastes of dates, and the toes of a dog. It worked as well as today's hair restorers. It was worthless too.

There is virtually no area involving health, sickness, virility, vanity, or fear of death where medical charlatans have not seen a profit. Miracle cures, wrinkle removers, sex treatments, pain relievers—the list is as long as human hope and gullibility can reach.

One might think that in this age of medical miracles and sophisticated technology quackery would be dead. Far from it. The quack has merely traded in his snake oil medicine for ''oral enzymes.'' He no longer operates from the back of a wagon or inside a tent but from a ''health clinic.'' His objective nevertheless remains the same—to play on people's health hopes and fears and part the hopeful and fearful from their money.

Medical fraud is booming. Quacks gross an estimated ten billion dollars a year. Victims are usually older persons. One California study revealed that of all medical frauds reported to the police, older persons were the victims in 70 percent of the cases. More money is actually wasted on quack ''cures'' than is invested in legitimate medical research. According to one study, for every dollar spent on legitimate arthritis research, twenty-five dollars is spent on fraudulent remedies.

How can you spot someone who practices medicine dishonestly or who offers worthless health aids for sale? How can you know which treatments are legitimate and which bogus? How can you decide between effective drugs and useless nostrums? legitimate devices and useless gadgetry? It is not easy. The quack even has a psychological edge. He or she will be telling you what you want to hear. And, often, a legitimate physician has to tell you hard, unpleasant truths that you don't want to hear.

Clues to Quackery

Still, there are a number of telltale clues that should put you on the alert to quackery. The quack often poses as a medical martyr who has found a miraculous cure, and the medical profession—out of greed, fear, or jealousy—has excluded the person. When you hear that story, watch out. You have met a quack.

Yet people are drawn to this line. Doctors do seem to have high incomes. Often they do disappoint us by their inability to cure or relieve a particular ailment. And, down through history, there are instances of the medical community's balking at new ideas. But that is not as likely today. Any physician, researcher, or scientist who finds a real cure for cancer, heart disease, or arthritis is going to be recognized by the medical profession, reap rewards from a grateful world population, and achieve immortality. He or she does not have to skulk around on the fringes of legitimate medicine. Therefore, when a so-called medical doctor starts demeaning other doctors as money grubbers, butchers, and sawbones in order to enhance himself or herself, beware. You have just seen the quack's warning flag.

Another surefire warning is if the doctor offers quick, miracle cures. Someone plagued with chronic pain who has gone from doctor to doctor without relief, for example, is an easy prey to someone who promises relief at last. But no legitimate medical practitioner will make such exaggerated claims to victims of chronic, debilitating diseases.

Some of the specific major health scams where the medical faker plies his or her trade are dealt with below and in the pages that follow.

Cancer Cures

The immunology treatment is only the latest form of cancer fraud. The American Cancer Society lists some seventy-five useless cancer treatments. Some are so preposterous that it seems unlikely that anyone would fall for them, but people do. One vicious promoter sold bottles of injectible seaweed and vitamin B-12 and doses of poisonous bacteria. The kit came complete with hypodermic needles and cost seven hundred dollars. Sad to say, it found buyers.

Before the immunology treatment, the great cancer fraud was Laetrile. The Laetrile treatment involved taking a substance concocted from apricot pits.

The National Cancer Institute has sponsored research to determine if Laetrile really has any value. One such study was carried out by the Mayo Clinic on 156 cancer patients for whom there was no standard treatment left. Laetrile failed to cure even one of these patients. Half of them died within five months; almost all the others died within a year. They would have survived just as long, the doctor concluded, with no treatment at all.

This discredited treatment has essentially been banned in the United States. Unfortunately, people still travel outside of the country to be treated with Laetrile.

Arthritis Cures

Twelve million Americans suffer from some form of arthritis. The disease offers a field day for the peddler of phony cures. Arthritis is chronic and can be excruciatingly painful. Desperate arthritis victims are understandably attracted to any nostrum that holds out relief. And the older person is the likeliest victim because arthritis is most common among older people.

Medical con artists have sold arthritis victims copper bracelets, radio-wave machines, iodized water, ''uranium'' gloves, and zinc discs to be worn in the shoes. None of these ''cures'' have succeeded at anything except making money for quacks.

Yet, you may run across arthritis sufferers who will swear by this or that pill, potion, or gadget. Are they imagining the effects? One explanation may be the placebo effect. The body and mind are strangely intertwined. Sometimes when you expect something to have a beneficial effect, it will—for a while. But the placebo effect is not likely to last if you are really sick. And it certainly is not going to cure you of arthritis.

Arthritis is also characterized by unpredictable remissions. For reasons not fully understood, the pain may temporarily go away. If the remission happens after you have tried a quack remedy, you may credit the remedy and start singing its praises to others.

Arthritis is tough enough for legitimate doctors to treat. Don't add false hopes and wasted money to the misfortune by being bilked by the quack's arthritis remedies.

Hearing-Aid Schemes

Most people experience some decline in hearing with advancing years. Nearly fifteen million Americans have some degree of hearing impairment. Medical con artists know this fact. And they are ready to turn it to their profit.

Beware of hearing-aid "consultants" who come to your door with their product. Legitimate medical aids are not sold that way. These charlatans will carry out fake tests and use scare tactics to convince you that you have a hearing problem. They will fast-talk you and high-pressure you to sign a sales contract on the spot. As one older victim testified, "I told the salesman I didn't think I needed a hearing aid. He insisted his tests showed my hearing would get worse, and later it would be too late to correct it."

Another trick is for the hearing-aid salesperson to cite an impressive list of satisfied customers, celebrities and firms who back their product. Don't be fooled. These unscrupulous people are not above inventing these endorsements.

Another favorite trick of hearing-aid hustlers is to offer free hearing tests at gathering places such as county fairs. Older people are again a favorite prey. If you are tested in such a place, you can soon expect a smooth-talking salesperson at your door ready to cure your hearing problem with his or her product. Turn a deaf ear.

You may indeed need a hearing aid. Real advances in hearing aids have been made, and they are a godsend to people afflicted with poor hearing. If you have a hearing problem, ask your family physician to recommend a competent audiologist. Or ask your local health department for references.

Comparison-shop for the best quality at the best price, just as you would any other expensive item. A reputable dealer will allow you reasonable time to check out the hearing aid and to decide if it is the right model for you. If not, an honest dealer will arrange either for an exchange or a refund. The hearing-aid fraud, on the other hand, will take your money and run. So deal with reputable, established firms that are going to be there when you need them. Avoid the consultant working out of a motel room, making "incredible" free offers, and giving "fabulous discount prices."

Deal only with honest professionals and you may be able to improve your hearing. Be careless and the sound you hear may be your money going down the drain.

Health Foods and Fads

The health and fitness movement that has swept the United States in recent years is admirable on the whole. But on occasion it has opened up new rackets for health charlatans. Take the expressions "health food" or "health food store." Isn't the produce in your supermarket health food? The same goes for the meat and dairy products. Aren't supermarkets "health stores"? Sometimes what you buy in a "health food store" is the same product you could obtain at a lower price in a conventional store.

All sorts of misleadingly labeled "food supplements" are on the market, for example, "oral enzymes" and "raw glandulars," products of questionable value. Raw glandulars are substances concocted of animal organs and are supposed to supplement your "weak organs." The quack will recommend raw pancreas supplement to strengthen your pancreas, raw heart supplement for your heart, or raw kidney supplement for your kidneys. These glandular supplements do nothing for your organs at all. They merely get digested in the stomach along with everything else you eat.

Diet Schemes

Nutritional scientists have made clear that there is only one way to lose weight. You must burn up more calories than you consume. And the only way to do so is to consume less food or to exercise more. Both in combination will work even faster. It is really a matter of mathematics. A pound of body weight is the equivalent of 3,500 calories. If, over the course of seven days, you cut your usual calorie consumption down by 500 calories per day, you will lose one pound that week. If you also exercise enough to burn up 500 more calories than usual each day, you will lose two pounds in that week. There is no magic to it, and there are no shortcuts.

Yet, people are perennially looking for ways to lose weight painlessly and quickly, without sacrifice and without effort. And, again, medical charlatans are ready to cash in on those futile hopes. One promoter promised to help people lose thirty pounds in thirty days. That's the equivalent of 3,500 calories a day! When one considers that a normal person consumes about 2,000 to 2,500 calories a day, the ridiculousness of this claim is evident. Yet, the promoter's ad brought in five thousand orders a day—at $22.50 each. That's $112,500.00 a day. And what did people get for their $22.50? A brochure describing the value of vitamins and exercise.

Another crew of sharp operators advertised a diet pill that would cause "rapid weight loss—without regard to food intake." The promoters claimed that the pill was endorsed by medical journals, based on clinical tests.

A pound of body weight is still 3,500 calories, and no pill that you take can alter that fact. Therefore, to lose weight without changing your eating habits, you would have to do it entirely through exercise—burning off 3,500 calories to lose one pound. A brisk walk lasting an hour would only burn off 215 calories. The offer was obviously a fraud. But that did not prevent seven thousand persons from spending good money for these phony diet pills.

Another huckster advertised, "Avoid fabulous doctor fees—lose weight by listening!" His method was a phonograph record, sold for $3.95, which supposedly planted hypnotic reducing suggestions in the listener's subconscious. People who bought the record became lighter by $3.95.

There are also all sorts of gadgets that are supposed to help you lose weight in a particular place—around the hips or off the thighs, for example. The "heat belt" is one such gadget. Such weight loss is called spot reducing. There is no such thing. There is no product, pill, or process that will remove fat from one part of the body alone. You lose weight proportionately from the entire body. To lose the five pounds you want off your stomach, you may have to lose twenty pounds of total body weight. The moral? Any offer for a spot-reducing aid is a phony.

Losing weight requires discipline and common sense. Do not follow any diet that offers exaggerated results in a short time. Do not follow a diet that does not involve balanced nutrition. And do not follow a diet that is not approved by qualified physicians and nutritionists. Otherwise, the only weight loss that you may experience will be from your wallet.

Government Protection

But doesn't the government protect us from worthless or possibly harmful medical and health products? Doesn't the Federal Trade Commission prohibit dishonest advertising? Doesn't the Food and Drug Administration shield us from worthless or even dangerous medical products?

The fact that a supposedly curative product is on the market is no guarantee that the government has tested it, approved it, and found it safe and effective. For the most part, these government agencies simply lack the staffs to keep up with the work load. When they do move, they tend to move slowly. Remember Carter's Little Liver Pills? It took the Federal Trade Commission over fifteen years to get the deceptive word *liver* out of that product's name.

The Food and Drug Administration is charged with enforcing the law that requires truth in labeling. On the whole, it does a good job. But the proliferation of health products is too great for the FDA to stay on top of the situation.

Health frauds continue to run the gamut of human hopes and fears. Here are two cases cited recently by the U.S. Senate Select Committee on Aging.

– A company initiated a nationwide campaign through the mail for a formula promising relief from prostate problems. Purchasers received a ninety-day supply of tablets that experts described as an irrational concoction of zinc, pumpkin seeds, and bee pollen. Over forty-two thousand people were victimized by this scheme. The company's take exceeded $420,000.

- Another company marketed—at ten dollars a bottle—an elixir that was guaranteed to "revitalize your sex life." Over thirty-six thousand people were conned by this scheme. The concoction was nothing more than a vitamin combination available at any drugstore at one-tenth the price.

Then there are "face peels" that are supposed to give you a youthful complexion, but which may scar your skin permanently. There are the bust-developer frauds, one of the oldest schemes. One older woman tells how at age fourteen she saved up her money and ordered a bust developer through the mail. She got back a pair of gloves.

Avoid wasting your money or risking your health on medical frauds.

DON'TS AND DOS

Don't

- believe in exaggerated claims and miracle cures.
- deal with so-called medical experts who claim that the medical profession is against their "cure."
- buy medical aids, substances, or advice from someone who comes to your door.
- be pressured into signing a contract for health equipment or services.
- accept the word of friends or neighbors about health cures. Check with your doctor.
- believe that all so-called health products have been tested or approved by the government just because they are on the market.

Do

- consult your family physician before buying or trying
any medical treatment, medicine, or health aid.
- consult your local Better Business Bureau or
consumer-protection agency about medical services
and products.
- have your hearing tested only by an audiologist.
- get your nutrition from a balanced diet, not from
questionable tonics and supplements.
- diet only by following a medically approved
weight-loss program.

6 *Mail Fraud*

Work-at-Home Offers

Viola and Earl E. lived in a trailer park community in the Southwest. Earl was a truck dispatcher who intended to retire at the end of the year. His retirement meant less income for them and a personal problem for Viola. Earl with nothing to do—and all day to do it in—would drive Viola crazy, she feared. Consequently, the ad in the newspaper seemed heaven-sent. "Earn Money in Your Spare Time at Home," it read. According to the ad, Viola could earn this money by sewing. She already had her own sewing machine and was a first-rate seamstress. And Earl could help her with the "business."

All that Viola had to do was pay a registration fee of fifteen dollars and submit a sample of her sewing so that the company could judge her skill. If her sample was found acceptable, Viola could expect to get work. Viola had no doubt that her sample could pass. So she sent in a sample of her embroidery along with the fee.

She never received an answer.

Viola was not alone. The newspaper ad that she responded to drew more than 200,000 persons. No one "qualified," and none of the money was returned.

Viola E. was a victim of postal fraud. Fraud that involves use of the mails is one of the most common forms of chicanery in the United States. The U.S. Postal Service has an Inspection Service of two thousand persons that spends about 25 percent of its time trying to prevent the kinds of mail fraud that ripped off Viola E.

According to the law, anyone using the mails for purposes of perpetrating fraud is committing a federal crime punishable by five years in jail, a $25,000 fine, or both. The penalties are evidently worth the risk to enough crooks because postal fraud continues to flourish. The President's Commission on Law Enforcement and the Administration of Justice estimates that over twice as many dollars are lost through various frauds than through robbery, burglary, and auto theft combined, and postal fraud accounts for a large share of the loss.

Viola E. was defrauded by the sew-at-home scheme. There are many variations—address envelopes at home, raise chinchillas, knit mittens, and so on. The ads are usually cleverly worded to sound like employment opportunities. But the tip-off is that you, in one form or another, have to send someone money first.

Contests

Not all contest offers that come through the mail are necessarily dishonest. But the odds of your winning even a legitimate contest are usually astronomical. Phony contests come in two kinds. In one form, you are notified by mail that you have already won a contest. What luck! You hadn't even entered it. In the other scheme, you are invited to take part in the contest. The requirements for entering are made so simple that there seems little reason not to try. What have you got to lose?

Here's what. By responding to such contest offers, you provide your name and address. Before you know it, you will find yourself on all sorts of mailing lists as a person susceptible to "glowing" offers. Some of these offers may prove misleading if not downright dishonest.

Here is an example. A retired English teacher got a piece of mail informing her that she had already won a prize in a nationwide contest. All that she had to do was sign an enclosed form showing her registration number and return it in the postage-paid envelope. The number would determine which prize she had won. First prize was a two-week vacation in Hawaii.

Shortly afterward, the former schoolteacher received her prize, a ball-point pen. Along with it was a brochure exclaiming, "Find Out How You Can Earn $20,000 with This Pen." The brochure went on to point out how all kinds of ordinary Americans were becoming best-selling authors by writing about their lives. All our schoolteacher had to do was send in $200 to receive an easy-to-follow outline for writing that best-seller. Once her manuscript was finished, she would then submit it to the editors. And, if her manuscript was chosen, her book royalties could quickly mount up—maybe to twenty thousand dollars in a few years.

Fortunately, as a former English teacher, the woman had a good idea of how legitimate publishers operate. And this was not one of them. The only writing that she did in response to this come-on was to send a complaint to the postal fraud authorities.

Real Estate Deals

Can you imagine people buying land that they have never seen through solicitation in the mail? They do it all the time, usually to their everlasting regret.

Fraudulent mail-order real estate deals usually offer land in sunny retirement climes—the South and Southwest. Retirees are a principal target. The brochure is likely to be handsome, the photographs of your prospective "dream house" stunning, and the promises irresistible. Nevertheless, be careful. Where land offers are concerned, if you haven't seen it, don't buy it. And certainly don't buy land strictly on the strength of a mail promotion.

Correspondence Courses

Turn to the back of your newspaper or magazine and you will likely find countless ways to improve yourself right at home, through the mail. Correspondence courses are offered that will make you a computer specialist, an artist, a cartoonist, or a real estate tycoon. You might think that older people would be immune to such appeals. But as retirement nears, many people begin to think of second careers or of supplementing their income.

Some of these offers are legitimate. Some are not. The problem is knowing which is which. If you respond to a correspondence ad and thereafter are bombarded with telephone calls and high-pressure tactics, be on your guard. A reputable school will not operate that way. And above all, don't sign a contract under pressure. It could prove costly, and you could have a hard time getting out of it. You should also be suspicious of promises of "high-paying jobs" if you enroll in the correspondence course.

In many states, people who offer correspondence courses have to be registered and approved by a government agency. Therefore, before enrolling in any such course, find out if it is on the level by calling someone in a position to know—your state education department, a local consumer-protection agency, or the Better Business Bureau.

Chain Referrals

Here is another variation on humanity's endless quest for something for nothing. You receive a beautiful brochure in the mail urging you to buy, say, a food processor. Here's the deal. Not only is it possible that this item will eventually cost you nothing, but you may even end up making a profit on the purchase. Here's how. Once you have the food processor, you are "authorized" to show it to your friends and neighbors. Thereafter, every time that one of them buys a processor, you get a commission. When you have had enough successful referrals, you will have paid for your machine, and any referrals beyond that are pure gravy.

So what's the catch? The deal isn't even necessarily illegal, except that legitimate manufacturers don't operate this way. Your mail-order machine is likely to be overpriced and not so hot either. The chances that you will make many successful referrals are slim. And if you do, all that you have really accomplished is to do the seller's work for him or her.

Medicine by Mail

One of the most despicable forms of fraud involves the selling of useless medicines or medical services by mail. Older persons are prime victims of such schemes. One mail-promoted fraud, for example, offered arthritis sufferers curative waters from Lourdes. Actually, the water came from a pool in California and could not cure a hangnail.

One particularly cruel medical mail fraud involved phony eye care. The promoters offered to cure glaucoma and near- and far-sightedness through eye exercises. Older people were told that if they sent for these exercises, they could throw away their glasses and glaucoma medicine. It seems inconceivable that anyone would encourage older persons to do something that could damage their eyesight—just to make money. It seems inconceivable, but it happened.

Another scam by mail offered a phony test for cancer, at a cost of ten dollars per test. Over fifteen thousand people fell for this fraud before the postal authorities shut it down.

If you are sick or need medicine, get help from your doctor, not your mailbox. Your health is too important to be risked on mail-order "bargains," miracle cures, and worthless tests.

Health Insurance

Health insurance for older people is commonly offered through the mail. Is it all suspect? No. Is some of this insurance fraudulent? Yes. For instance, a World War II veteran received an official-looking envelope in the mail from the Veteran's Insurance Division. The letter inside began "Dear Veteran." It stated that the recipient qualified for a special ten-thousand-dollar life insurance policy at the same premiums that he had paid when he was a GI—over forty years before. The man assumed that the offer came from the government as a service to veterans. So he signed the enclosed forms and mailed them back.

The government had nothing to do with this offer. The insurance was being sold by private promoters. The rates were indeed the same as the veteran had paid years before. But the fine print whittled down the benefits almost to the point of worthlessness.

The "veteran" pitch is one of a number used by unscrupulous people to sell older people insurance. Other promoters drop the names of religious groups, clubs, unions, and fraternal organizations though the insurance does not necessarily have their endorsement.

And watch out for the mail-order insurance policy that offers "low, low premiums" of "only pennies a day." At ninety-nine pennies a day, you would wind up paying over $360 a year for insurance of possibly zero value.

The postal service has also had to move against insurance promoters who have defrauded older people by selling them unnecessary Medicare insurance through the mail. In one case, the inspectors found that several older people in Massachusetts had spent as much as forty thousand dollars for worthless insurance. One woman, aged ninety-three, had been sold maternity insurance.

If an insurance promotion received in the mail interests you, check it out first. Ask your state insurance department, local consumer-protection agency, or the Better Business Bureau for guidance.

Postal Service Protection

Since the inspection unit of the U.S. Postal Service spends three-quarters of its time on other matters, it obviously cannot stop the flood tide of mail-order fraud. Even when the service is on to a scheme, it must prove "fraudulent intent," a time-consuming and difficult charge. Furthermore, even if the postal inspectors do put a swindler out of business, they do not have the power to recover your money.

Do not fall for any claims that a product has been endorsed by the postal service or by any other federal agency just because it is offered through the mail. The government does not endorse products.

Your best defense against postal fraud is common sense, a sharp eye, and healthy skepticism toward questionable offers. If you do feel that you have come across a deceitful and dishonest mail-order scheme, report it to your post office. Postal con artists are like chameleons, popping up again and again in a dozen different guises. Anything that you can do to help the postal authorities find them and convict them is a service to your community and to yourself.

DON'TS AND DOS

Don't

- trust make-money-at-home schemes requiring you to send money.
- assume that all contests through the mail are legitimate.
- buy land sight unseen through the mail.
- be taken in by chain-referral sales schemes.
- believe in medical cures offered through the mail.
- buy insurance through the mail without checking with authorities first.
- believe that products or services offered through the mail are approved by the U.S. Postal Service.

Do

- check out real estate offers by mail with your state regulating authority, local consumer-protection agency, or Better Business Bureau.
- check out mail-order correspondence courses with your state education department, local consumer-protection agency, or Better Business Bureau.
- check out any medical products or services offered by mail with your doctor before buying.
- check out insurance offered by mail with your state insurance department, local consumer-protection agency, or Better Business Bureau.
- report evidence of mail fraud to your post office.

7 *Consumer Fraud*

Real Estate

Howard and Sarah Z. had long dreamed of leaving the Northeast, where they had spent all their lives, and moving to the warmer Southwest as soon as Howard sold his dry-cleaning business. Sarah suffered from rheumatism, and the cold northern winters had become increasingly hard on her. Howard often thought about the move and imagined himself taking up golf in some sunny clime.

Consequently, when the couple received a telephone call informing them that they had been invited to a free dinner followed by a film on "Retirement Edens" at a local motel-restaurant, they were immediately intrigued.

At the dinner were nearly seventy-five persons about Howard's and Sarah's age. On their arrival, they were greeted by a stylish young woman named Nan and an exuberant young man named Ken. Nan and Ken also provided them with handsome, four-color brochures containing photographs of a lush retirement community set in a breathtaking Arizona landscape.

After the dinner, the guests were shown a film featuring "Everfair Estates." Howard and Sarah smiled at each other knowingly as they watched it. Their own town was then shivering under near-zero temperatures. The streets were covered with soot-blackened snow. But Everfair Estates gleamed in perpetual sunshine. Besides the ranch-style houses, the film showed a golf course, tennis courts, an Olympic-sized pool, riding trails, a well-stocked lake, and a clubhouse. Inside the clubhouse were an indoor pool, whirlpool baths, a steam room, and a sauna.

After the movie, Nan and Ken told everyone how they could become homeowners in Everfair Estates. They explained that the community had been planned down to the last detail for comfort and convenience but that it was still in the building stage. Once the community was completed, prices would increase substantially. Therefore, Howard and Sarah and the others could reap huge discounts by buying now and getting in on the ground floor. The later price was going to be four thousand dollars an acre. But ''charter buyers'' could get in for three thousand dollars.

One man asked Nan and Ken a lot of tough questions. He was obviously not the type to be sold a bill of goods. He impressed Howard and Sarah. But finally the man said, ''You've convinced me. I know a good deal when I see one.'' After he signed up, several others did too. Howard and Sarah again smiled at each other and bought a ten-acre tract at Everfair Estates. Howard eventually had to take out a loan on his business to meet the payments.

A year later, Howard was ready to sell the dry-cleaning business. He and Sarah made a trip to Arizona to see their property and to start working with the developer on their home.

The trip was one of the most shattering experiences of their lives. Everfair Estates turned out to be thousands of acres of scrub growth and desert. There was no lake, no golf course, no pool, no clubhouse, and not a single home. The nearest water was straight down, seven hundred feet below the ground.

The word ''planned,'' it turned out, was the key to Everfair Estates. Everything promised was still in the ''planning'' stage. The developers had not yet even obtained the necessary legal approvals to have housing built on this trackless wasteland. Everfair Estates existed only in the brochures and promotional material. Even the pictures of a sun-filled community shown in the brochure and the movie had been taken somewhere else. Howard and Sarah had traded their retirement nest egg for a worthless patch of sand.

It was ironic. Howard and Sarah had often expressed their fear of street crime where they lived. As a small businessman, Howard was well aware of burglaries, stickups, and robberies. Yet, the odds that he and his wife would fall victim to a violent crime were far lower than that they would be bilked by white-collar criminals, as they were. As government studies show, for every dollar of loss in violent crime, two dollars are lost to fraud. In short, far too little attention is paid to this likeliest source of victimization of older people.

The reasons for the lack of sufficient attention are many. Violent crimes grab the headlines. Violent crimes can be life-and-death matters. Frauds, on the other hand, are usually not even reported by the victims. Many people are too embarrassed to admit that they have been taken. Often they are not even sure that a crime has been committed. The contracts that Howard and Sarah signed were technically legal, if not ethical. Careful wording got around the fact that the community existed only on paper.

Economic thievery has devastating effects on older people. Most people have a certain degree of anxiety about how secure they will be in their old age. They want to be reasonably self-sufficient, to enjoy lives of dignity and not be burdens on their children. The loss of hard-won dollars in the later years risks all this. Consequently, while you may fear violent crime, you should show just as much intelligent concern over the crimes that are more likely to victimize you, fraud and deception. Borderline schemes may be technically legal but can victimize you nonetheless. There are many pitfalls in the marketplace.

The biggest mistake that Howard and Sarah Z. made was that they bought real estate "site unseen." It seems an obvious precaution to see land offered for sale first. But the number of people who will plunk down hard-earned money on real estate that they have never laid eyes on is astonishing. In one California land scheme over five hundred buyers paid $2,000 an acre for worthless land, and not *one* of them had visited the site first.

When customers are foolish enough, land speculators can make money even without being dishonest. You may, for example, be drawn by an ad for land in a sunny part of the country going for "only $350 an acre." You buy into the deal only to find out later that the site is virtually inaccessible and that you could have bought land there for $30 an acre.

Or take the case of one speculator who bought land in the Southwest for $700 an acre. He advertised the sites in Eastern newspapers as "dream plots" and sold them for $6,200 an acre. Nobody in his or her right mind would have bought this land had they seen it first. People were buying the ad, not the land. Or as in Howard and Sarah's case, they bought a movie and a slick sales pitch. Even the tough customer who asked the hard questions at their free dinner was a plant, someone working with the promoters.

Failure to see the land first has resulted in terribly cruel deceptions. Authorities report one case in which a man was bilked of thirty thousand dollars by promoters who sold him land in Florida that was underwater. His money had come from a reparations settlement for surviving the Dachau concentration camp during the Holocaust.

Be especially alert to promoters offering contests, free vacations, and other similar enticements. Don't believe that what you see in the brochures and movies is what you are buying. Read every word of the sales contract. Check with your bank about the proposed financing. Try to get some idea of what nearby property is selling for. If you feel that you are being high-pressured, stop, look, and be careful. Don't be rushed into a major investment no matter how tempting the bait dangled in front of you. And, never ever buy real estate that you have not seen. Here, seeing is truly believing.

Many states do have programs to regulate the sale of real estate. Their jurisdiction, however, does not run beyond their borders, and it is difficult for them to police all the land schemes promoted through advertising, the mail, and even by telephone. Nevertheless, take advantage of what protection does exist. Before you think seriously about any out-of-state real estate investment, check it out with your state's real estate regulating agency.

Financial Finagling

Without credit, our economy would collapse and our standard of living plummet. If people had to pay cash for new cars and new homes, Detroit would become a ghost town overnight, and the forests would largely be safe from the lumberman's ax. The magic of credit is to have now what one can only afford tomorrow.

The decision when to borrow, for what, and how much are individual judgments that only the consumer can make. And only the consumer can avoid dishonest or misleading credit schemes. Some of these schemes are not illegal, but they are tricky.

Take, for example, the balloon note. You sign an installment contract to buy a new car. You are particularly attracted by the low monthly payments. What you fail to notice in the fine print is that the final installment is far larger than the others. That's the "balloon." It makes possible the lower earlier payments. But if you cannot meet that final payment, your car can be repossessed. Not only that, but you may end up losing all the money that you paid in so far. Before falling for those low monthly payments, make sure you can manage to cover the whopper payment at the end.

Another form of legal but potentially costly financing is debt consolidation. Given the ease of credit today, people often get in over their heads. If your debts seem overwhelming, you may be attracted by the outfit that offers to lump all your bills together while you just pay them one monthly payment lower than the sum of all your present payments. Be careful. You could wind up worse off than you were before. Even though the single monthly payment is lower, you may find yourself paying a much higher interest rate and making payments for a far longer time.

If your debts are getting out of hand, sit down with your bank or savings and loan people and ask for their help. Legitimate lending institutions do have plans for helping you consolidate your debts and working out payments that you can manage better. But be wary of the high-promise, high-pressure, low-payment debt consolidator.

How about the ad offering "Loans up to $1,000—with no interest"? Have lenders become Santa Claus? When you borrow from these outfits, you sign a note for a thousand dollars, but you get considerably less cash in hand. The interest and other charges have merely been subtracted in advance.

Why would people fall for an interest-free loan? Need may be the answer. But another reason is the failure to use common sense. Lenders are in the business to make money. If they charge no interest, they make no money. If you think about it that way, you know that there has to be a catch. Find out that catch before you fall for the scheme.

Bait and Switch

In bait and switch, you are lured with one offer and then maneuvered to something else. You go for the advertised bait and get the unadvertised hook, like any poor fish. There are several kinds of bait advertising that are likely to be dangled before you.

For example, on television, over the radio, or in your newspaper, you learn of a sewing machine being offered at an irresistibly low price. The machine bears a respectable brand name. The sale ends this weekend. You quickly get yourself down to the dealer.

Evidently others had the same idea because the clerk tells you that the advertised machine is all sold out. You are disappointed. You ask when they are likely to get another shipment in. "There won't be any more," he sadly informs you. Then his smile brightens. "But that model wasn't really all that great. In fact, the manufacturer is discontinuing it. That's why the price was so low." But, it turns out, the store has another machine, same manufacturer but a far superior model, that is also on sale. It is not the same low price as the advertised machine. But when you compare the monthly payments, it's only a few dollars more.

You made all that effort to get out to the shopping center. They don't have the machine you wanted, but here is another bargain and an even better model. The dealer has put you in the psychological frame to buy. You agree to take the second, more expensive machine. You have been baited and switched.

In many areas, bait advertising has been outlawed. That does not mean it never happens. When it does, you first have to bring a formal complaint against the advertiser. How many consumers are going to take the time to do that? Next, the charge has to be proved. It must be established that there was no real effort on the part of the seller to sell the "bargain" merchandise. These legal fine points are hard to establish. You are a consumer, not a lawyer. Consequently, prosecutions are few, and bait advertising continues its long, disreputable history.

Here is another form of bait and switch. You see an ad on television offering a three-piece bedroom suite at a bargain price. The furniture looks fine on your screen. The low price is made to seem reasonable through the use of phrases like "manufacturer's overstock" or "warehouse clearance sale."

You hurry to the furniture store. When you see the advertised suite, you are disappointed. It is poorly made. The clerk appears to be in your corner too. He is embarrassed to sell such shoddy goods, he says, but they have a lovely, high-quality suite that you ought to look at as long as you are there. It's bait and switch again—not necessarily illegal, just sleazy.

Are you a bargain hunter who likes "scratch and dent" sales? Nothing wrong with that if the chair with the uneven legs and the lamp with the crack are not simply come-ons. But once the clerk starts knocking the sale items and tries to lure you to high-priced merchandise, you are getting the bait-and-switch routine.

Another form of bait is the "nailed to the floor" item. The merchandise is not literally nailed to the floor, but it might as well be because the merchant has no intention of selling it. The store may have advertised a lamp at an unbelievable price. But when you get there, you find out that the lamp is "a floor model," the only one left and not for sale. Or it has a "Sold" tag on it. "But we do have another lovely lamp, only a little more expensive." Watch out. Here comes the bait and switch.

There are two things that you can do about bait-and-switch advertising: One is to be aware of it so that you don't fall for it. The other is to report it to your local consumer-protection agency or Better Business Bureau. If you live in a state where the practice is illegal, there may be grounds for prosecution. At the very least, a sufficient number of complaints may create enough pressure on the merchant to stop the practice.

Going Out of Business Sales

Do you remember that marvelous old cartoon? A man is standing in front of a store. He has his arm around a little boy. The storefront is plastered with signs—Going Out of Business, Forced to Liquidate, Lost Our Lease, Everything Below Cost. The man looks fondly at the little boy and says, "Just think, Junior, when you grow up, the store will be yours."

We have all seen these kinds of stores, particularly in big cities. Again, outright fraud is hard to prove in such cases. The buyer's best defense is caution and skepticism. Merchandise being offered at or below cost defies reason. Nobody is in business to lose money. And sales in such stores are likely to be for cash only and no refunds, please. Once you buy, you are stuck.

Franchise and Distributorship Schemes

Business franchises are tempting to retired people who may have spent a lifetime working for someone else and now want to be their own boss. The opportunities are endless—from hamburgers to motels and from picture framing to pizzas. And we know that, for many people, franchises have been the route to riches, or at least a comfortable income.

Because the words *franchise* and *distributorship* now have a golden ring to them, hustlers have moved into the territory. Several fraudulent schemes have popped up in the thriving health and fitness field. Prospective franchisees are lured by offers of high profits, guaranteed customers, and advertising and promotional support. They may even be assured that unsold merchandise will be bought back if the franchisee is unhappy with the arrangement or if sales don't pan out. The deal seems goof-proof. But what can happen in reality?

In West Virginia, a man bought a distributorship to supply pharmaceutical products to ten stores. He paid ninety-nine hundred dollars for the distributorship. The company selling him the distributorship was to arrange sales with the ten stores. All the distributor had to do was deliver the merchandise. The company took the man's money, delivered inadequate products, and supplied no customers. The fellow had to hire a lawyer to get his investment back.

A Pennsylvania couple responded to an ad in a fishing magazine offering to set up investors in fishing tackle dealerships. The couple met with the president of the company, who explained what they would get as dealers: a money-back guarantee if the business failed, exchange of slow-selling tackle for faster-moving items, a computerized system for locating the best fishing lures, advertising in national magazines, market research, and the lowest prices available for tackle equipment. Lured by these glowing promises, the couple invested eleven thousand dollars in the fishing tackle dealership. The company failed to come through on even one of its promises. The venture was a total loss for the investor.

In another distributorship scheme, a pair of California operators sold distributorships in special boards and pads. These boards and pads supposedly emitted negative ions, which the body would absorb during sleep. The treatment supposedly relieved pain, tension, and insomnia. The promoters promised potential earnings of forty thousand dollars a year. No distributor made anywhere near that figure. The company promised to supply customers. It supplied none. And it reneged on its buy-back guarantee. The casualties? Sixty-three "distributors" were defrauded of over $307,000.

In the above examples, you can see the repeated promises running through phony franchise and distributorship schemes: high profits, quality merchandise, guaranteed customers, assistance in advertising the product, and buy-back promises. Whenever anyone puts a business proposition to you that "can't fail," watch out. Don't accept promises at face value. Before investing, check with your local consumer-protection agency, the Better Business Bureau, your bank, or a lawyer. Ask the promoters for the names of other distributors whom you can talk to about their experiences.

Phony Advertising Campaigns

The sharp operator always has a plausible reason to explain his or her hustle. You can buy this marvelous vacuum cleaner, for example, at a huge discount because your involvement is going to be used in promoting the product.

Everyone wants to feel like an insider who is getting preferred treatment. So you bite. But, all too often, the advertising campaign is a phony intended to get you to sign a contract for a product or a service that is overrated and overpriced. The best move you can make is to check with your local consumer-protection agency or Better Business Bureau to find out about the outfit's reputation before committing yourself.

Freezer Food Plans

We all know that it makes sense to buy food, such as meat, in quantity when it is on special and keep it in the freezer. That's why commercial freezer food plans sound so appealing. And honest plans offer real opportunities for you to economize.

But there are freezer food plan operators who can give you a chilling experience. They promise you a plan that will "pay for itself." After you sign up, you find that you bought an overpriced freezer at high interest payments and possibly inferior food that you do not want or will not use.

Care with Contracts

When you buy anything—a freezer, an automobile, a lawn care service—on the installment plan, you have to sign a contract. You also sign a contract when you borrow money, purchase insurance, or subscribe to a magazine. The contract is a written document setting forth the terms agreed to by the parties who sign it. And contracts are enforceable by law.

The important point when signing a contract is to understand what you are agreeing to. The smooth talker who sells an overpriced hearing aid to an older person who doesn't need it may use a perfectly legal sales contract. Once you sign it, you may have no choice but to meet the terms of that contract.

Consequently, never sign anything until you have read it and understand it. If you have any questions—if the language is confusing or the print too fine—don't sign until you have someone you trust check out the contract. That person may be a lawyer, someone at your bank, or a friend who knows more about such matters than you do. The delay will save you from making costly mistakes and will likely scare off a dishonest promoter.

If the seller tries to pressure you into signing right away because "the offer is about to run out," or the seller uses any other high-pressure tactics, be careful. You have just seen a consumer warning light flash on. Also, never sign a contract that has blank spaces in it. That's almost as risky as signing a blank check. And when you do sign, make sure that you get a copy of the contract and that it is also signed by the seller.

Some states allow a cancellation period in sales contracts. If you find something misleading or deceptive in a contract, you have a certain period—say, three days—during which you can cancel it. If you feel unhappy or suspicious about a sales contract that you have signed, contact your local consumer-protection agency or Better Business Bureau and find out if your state offers you this right to cancel.

You should also understand any warranties or guarantees given with a product. Do you really know what the seller is guaranteeing? For how long? Under what conditions? The fine print in a warranty or guarantee may taketh away what the big print giveth. So read and make sure that you understand guarantees and warranties *before* you buy.

Deeds of Trust

Ownership of a home is the bedrock of many people's lives. If you are older, your home may be your ultimate resource. Anything that threatens home ownership may threaten a secure retirement.

One vicious practice involving contracts that can threaten home ownership is the "deed of trust." Many people have been tricked into signing contracts that contain a deed of trust pledging their home as security for the contract. One older woman believed that she was signing a receipt for a television set. Instead, she had signed a sales contract for the set secured by a deed of trust on her home.

In another case, a man had some relatively minor repairs performed on his house. He signed a contract for the work. The man became ill and could not keep up his payments on the contract. The contract was thereafter sold to a finance company and secured by a deed of trust.

In each of these cases, default on the contract could have meant the loss of the older person's home. What is the answer? Read carefully anything that is put in front of you to sign. Better still, get outside advice before you sign.

The Inflated Trade-in

Your car has 102,000 miles on it, has bald tires, and burns almost as much oil as gas. It's time to trade it in. You do a little checking and find that the "Blue Book" lists your car's value at four hundred dollars.

You go to an automobile dealer and find the new car that you like. The salesperson starts talking trade-in. He asks what you are driving. You tell him. He says he can get you a thousand dollars for your old car. You can hardly believe your good fortune.

"Just a minute," he smiles. "Let me make sure I can get the boss to okay that."

While you wait, you are itching to own that new car gleaming in the lot. Finally, the salesperson comes back, a bit shamefaced. "The boss says no way! I tried, but I couldn't convince him to go for a thousand dollars."

The psychological trap has now been set. He is just waiting for you to spring it. And you do when you ask, "Then how much can you give me for my car?"

The business about getting the boss's approval of that inflated trade-in was only a trick to hook you. The car business is full of such behavior. If deceit is used in hooking you in the first place, is this the place where you should be buying a car? Can you trust any other claims made here? What kind of service can you expect from this kind of dealer? An automobile is a heavy investment. You should have as much confidence in the dealer as you do in the car.

Car-Repair Schemes

Every lucky car owner has an "Earl." Earl is the guy at the garage where you have taken your car for years. He is a born tinkerer, honest as daylight, and you wouldn't have anybody else touch your car. Unfortunately, not all of us have an Earl, or we move and have to start looking for a new mechanic, or we are on the road when trouble happens.

What goes on under the hood still remains an utter mystery to many motorists. Consequently, many are at the mercy of mechanics. An automobile is a complex piece of machinery, and people pretty much have to depend on what the "experts" tell them is wrong with it. They have to hope that the mechanic is honest and competent. Not all of them are. You may not be able to tell a distributor cap from a hub cap, but here are some common auto repair scams to watch out for.

You are driving far from home and pull into a station for gas. The attendant asks if you want your oil checked. You say yes. The attendant opens the hood and proceeds to "short-stick" you. That is, he or she doesn't push the dipstick all the way in and tells you that you are low on oil. You agree to let the attendant add a quart. Not only have you bought an unnecessary quart of oil, but also there is danger of an oil overflow doing damage once you get back on the road. The best protection in such situations is to get out of the car while it is being serviced. If you stand next to the attendant, he or she is less likely to try any funny business.

Another fairly common trick is for an attendant to cut your fan belt and then show you the "worn-out" belt. You unwittingly buy a new fan belt.

There is a whole bag of tricks that the crooked mechanic knows, for example, Alka-Seltzer dropped into a battery cylinder to make it foam. "You sure need a new battery," the mechanic says. A squirt of steak sauce smoking on a hot engine manifold might convince you that you need a new fuel pump. Or you head for a rest room while the attendant is gassing up the car, and when you get back, he or she shows you that one of your tires is leaking (the attendant started the leak). But you're in luck. The station has a terrific special on radials that week.

Or, the mechanic puts your car up on the hoist and shakes the front wheels. "Loose," the mechanic says. "You got worn ball joints." You never heard of ball joints. And you don't know that they are *supposed* to have a little play in them. But you don't want to take a chance on the road with your grandchild in the car. So you let the mechanic make an unnecessary repair. Your cost, seventy-five dollars.

Car-loving Americans spend nearly thirty billion dollars a year to service and repair their automobiles. How much of that work is honestly and competently performed? The American Automobile Association tried to find out through a survey in one midwestern city. They studied two thousand repair jobs and discovered that in approximately one out of three cases the work was improperly performed.

What can you do to avoid roadside rackets or dishonest mechanics? One precaution is to get out of the car and keep an eye on the attendant when gassing up at a strange place. For any repair work anywhere, always insist on a written estimate. Before you pay, make sure that the bill contains a detailed, itemized list of the work performed.

In the past generation, this country has experienced a consumer revolution. Local consumer-protection agencies rarely existed twenty years ago. Yet, no consumer agency can help you if you don't help yourself first. You have to be alert to rip-offs in order to recognize and report them. There is a fuzzy line between outright criminality and merely deceptive or misleading acts. You can't always count on protective agencies to bail you out. In the end, the best consumer advocate you can have is yourself. Your own common sense, coupled with good information, is the surest protection against being bilked.

DON'TS AND DOS

Don't
- buy retirement real estate until you have seen it.
- buy retirement real estate under high-pressure, "sign right away" conditions.
- buy retirement real estate without checking out the seller.
- fall for "interest-free" loan schemes.
- be fooled by advertising that baits you with one product while the salesperson tries to switch you to another.

    – sign up for a franchise or distributorship under
      high-pressure tactics.

    – fall for bargains hitched to so-called advertising
      campaigns.

    – sign a contract without reading it.

    – sign a contract with empty spaces in it.

    – sign a contract secured by a deed of trust on your
      home.

    – be fooled by a high trade-in offer on your car that is
      later disapproved by the "boss."

    – leave your car unattended when you pull into a service
      station.

Do

    –check out real estate retirement proposals with
      competent experts before signing.

    – make price comparisons of nearby land before buying
      into retirement real estate plans.

    – report suspected real estate swindles to the proper
      authorities.

    – watch out for installment purchase contracts containing
      a big final balloon payment.

    – compare terms of debt-consolidation promoters with
      the same service at your bank or savings and loan
      association.

    – report suspected bait advertising to consumer
      authorities.

    – be leery of "going out of business" sales.

    – get an independent opinion of franchise or
      distributorship offers before buying in.

    – read all sales contracts with care, especially the fine
      print.

    – know what is being guaranteed or warranted, for how
      long, and under what terms before you buy
      a product.

    – find out if your state allows a cancellation period for
      sales contracts.

    – get out of your car where you can watch the attendant
      when gassing up at unfamiliar stations.

    – get a written estimate before consenting to car repairs.

    – get a detailed, itemized bill for all car repairs.

8 *Rape and Assault*

Maria D., a woman living alone in Los Angeles, was awakened by someone banging on her door in the middle of the night. She hesitated to open the door and asked, "Who is it?" A frenzied voice responded that he was the man next door. Maria recognized his voice, though she did not know this person well. He said that he had to use her phone. Maria was afraid that he might break down the door, so she let him in. He raped her.

The panic, humiliation, and injury caused by this act was only the beginning of Maria's ordeal. She was the chief prosecution witness at the rapist's trial, where she was compelled to relive the nightmare. She had to endure cross-examination by an aggressive young defense counsel, who kept insinuating that Maria, who had been married for fifty years, did not understand the elements of intercourse and rape. Furthermore, Maria lived in terror for weeks during the trial because her tormenter, who was free on bail, was still living next door to her.

Maria D. was a victim of rape, defined formally as "the carnal knowledge of a female forcibly and against her will."

The crimes discussed thus far in this book are crimes designed one way or another to part you from your money or possessions. The means may be violent, deceitful, dangerous, or merely unethical. The weapons may be force or lies. In any case, the ultimate object is the criminal's enrichment at your expense.

There are other crimes that begin as robberies or burglaries and end up as acts of physical violence, such as rape, aggravated assault, and homicide. There are also vicious, twisted, and sick personalities whose perverse fulfillment is to do you harm. It may seem that there is little an older woman can do when confronted by a rapist or that an older man can do when confronted by a vicious thug. But there are some sensible precautions you can take.

Statistically, it is possible that you may be struck by lightning, but the odds are so remote that you waste little of your life worrying about this danger. By the same token, knowing the actual odds against your being physically assaulted should provide you with a certain peace of mind without making you overly careless. When put into realistic perspective, some crimes can be dealt with intelligently.

Rape

In 1981, according to the National Crime Survey, 178,000 women may have been raped. The estimate is imprecise because rape is one of the least reported crimes. The National Crime Survey estimates that something like 45 percent of all rapes are not reported to the police. Other authorities find this figure far too conservative. Perhaps as many as two of every thousand women in this country are raped in a typical year.

Who is raped? Most rape victims are young. Women most likely to be raped are aged twenty-four or less. Those least likely to be raped are sixty or older. A young woman aged sixteen to nineteen stands twenty-seven more chances of being raped than does a woman of sixty. But statistical odds are of small consolation to the older woman who actually is raped.

Who are the rapists? It is impossible to profile "typical" rapists except to say that most of them are young, usually thirty or under. They cut across all racial lines. They are likely to be of average or above-average intelligence. They may be drifters or successful professionals, single or married men with children. Whatever the deceptive exterior, the rapist likely experienced a childhood marked by cruelty or brutality. He is often insecure and sees the act of rape as an expression of power or masculinity.

Although it is difficult to profile the rapist, it is possible to profile his crime. The following conclusions are based on studies conducted in New York City and Philadelphia of rape victims and from other information supplied by convicted rapists.

- Two out of three rapes were associated with another crime such as robbery or burglary.
- About 75 percent of all victims were raped in their own homes.
- About 50 percent of the victims lived alone.
- About half of the rapes occurred during daylight.
- One victim out of three knew the rapist.
- In one rape out of three, the assailant entered the victim's house through an unlocked door or window.
- In one rape out of two, the woman had admitted the assailant into her home.

Where does most rape occur geographically? The crime is perpetrated about twice as often in big cities as in small towns or rural areas. The rape rate in suburbia falls somewhere in between. The incidence of reported rape has increased substantially over the past two decades and went up nearly 75 percent between 1971 and 1981. Not until 1983 did the incidence of rape decrease—by 1 percent.

Since rape is such a vicious crime, why do women so often fail to report it? The answers are many: embarrassment, fear of reprisal by the rapist, the possible reaction of husband or boyfriend, and feelings of guilt. One way or another, the victim's reluctance to talk stems from the great body of public misinformation and misunderstanding about rape. It is a crime clouded by ignorance, prejudice, and distortion and surrounded with myths.

Myth 1: The rapist rapes for sex. Wrong. Virtually the only thing sexual about rape is the organs involved. Rape is an act of violence. The rapist is usually trying to express hostility, hatred, or a twisted idea of masculinity.

Myth 2: Women want to be raped. Dead wrong. This perverted notion is one of the most vicious myths associated with rape. It confuses sexual violence and sexual pleasure. The loving, caring, affectionate feelings that a normal woman associates with sex are not satisfied by the forcible violation of her body.

Myth 3: A woman can easily prevent herself from being raped. Untrue and unfair. How many men with a gun to their heads are going to resist handing over a wallet to a mugger? By the same token, can we expect a woman with a knife against her throat to risk her life by resisting a psychopath? There may be situations in which a woman can resist rape. But to suggest that a woman can easily elude a rapist is nonsense.

Myth 4: Women provoke rape. This distorted reasoning says that a woman—by her dress, manner, or speech—invites rape. Such thinking is in the same league with a conclusion that a well-dressed, obviously prosperous man invites and deserves a robbery and a beating.

Myth 5: Rape usually occurs between strangers. Not necessarily so. Studies show that women often know their assailants. Some researchers have found that half the time the rapist is a friend, an acquaintance, or a family member.

How can an older woman protect herself from this assault?

Preventive Measures to Take

Home security precautions are the first line of defense against rape. These precautions are essentially the same as recommended for keeping your house or apartment burglarproof. In a New York–Philadelphia study, one out of three victims had been raped by someone who came through an unlocked door or window. The importance of having good locks on your doors and windows cannot be emphasized too strongly.

Also, don't advertise the fact that you live alone. List yourself in the phone book not as Anna May Bates, but as A. M. Bates. Do the same on your mailbox. And never open your door to a stranger before determining that there is a legitimate purpose to the visit. Remember Maria D.? She opened the door because her neighbor said he had to use the telephone. She was put off her guard because she knew the man. But if a stranger should come to your door and ask to use the telephone, say that you would be happy to make the call for him. And leave him waiting on the other side of the door.

When your door bell rings, you might call out, "I'll get it, George," or something similar suggesting that you are not alone. Ask who it is before opening the door. It is even risky to open a chain-locked door, since an intruder can force these locks with a quick lunge.

A woman living alone should keep a telephone near her bed and have telephone numbers available, such as those of the police, the building superintendent, or a friend who can be called in an emergency. Call at the first sign of trouble. Better to be too cautious than too trusting.

While many rapes occur in the victim's home, there are other risky areas. They are the same places that you have been advised to avoid to prevent your being robbed—deserted streets at night, deserted laundry rooms in your building, parks, school grounds, and parking garages. Be careful about getting into an elevator with a strange man. If it is unavoidable, stay close to the control panel so that if a rape is attempted, you can hit the floor buttons and the emergency button.

Car security precautions can thwart rapists as well as thieves. Keep your car door locked at all times and your windows rolled up so that an assailant cannot reach into your car. Before getting into your car, check the inside to make sure that no one is hiding in it. Do not accept rides from strangers or pick up hitchhikers. When you arrive home, have your house key ready to shorten the time you spend in the vestibule or entranceway.

When you leave the house, try to do so with a friend. Avoid walking through groups of loitering men or boys. Cross the street to avoid such confrontations. If a slow-moving car pulls up alongside you, cross the street, reverse your direction, go into a store, or seek someone's help.

Resistance to Rape

If you have taken all reasonable precautions and are nevertheless threatened with rape, should you resist? submit? flee? scream? It would be irresponsible for anyone to endorse a single response for all situations. There are no such hard-and-fast rules where rape is concerned. The best advice that can be offered is the considered judgment of police officers who deal with the problem and the word of rapists themselves, since a good deal of research has been done with them to determine what makes them tick and how they operate.

Based on information from those sources, aggressive resistance is not usually recommended for the older rape victim. A woman who is good-sized, healthy, strong, and skilled in self-defense may fight back successfully under certain circumstances. But several convicted rapists who assaulted women over age fifty said, during interviews, that fighting back was likely to result in serious injury to the victim. Most law-enforcement officers agree.

If you are attacked outside your home and there is a likelihood that you will be heard, your best defense may be to scream. Your screaming may surprise the rapist, cause him to flee, or distract him long enough for you to get away. And scream as soon as you sense the attack. The rapist is going to try to get you to the ground, and once that happens, your chances of escaping are reduced.

Some experts suggest shouting ''Fire!'' when you are assaulted rather than ''Help!'' ''Rape!'' or ''Police!'' The latter three words may provoke your assailant to shut you up by violent means, and you could be seriously hurt. Also, sad to say, people who hear you may be more inclined to respond to a yell of ''Fire!'' Yells of ''Police!'' or ''Rape!'' signal violence, and some people will resist becoming involved.

If in a particular situation you think that resistance may save you or gain time for you to escape, go for the rapist's genitals or his eyes. These are his most vulnerable spots. Use your nails or fists or any sharp object you can get your hands on, such as an umbrella, a pen, or a pencil. Scratch, kick, and bite. If he grabs you, try to drive your heel into his foot.

It is unfortunate that no book can give clear-cut advice in the event you are attacked by a rapist. But, rapists are individuals, each of whom may act differently. And there are different environments. The rape may be attempted in your home, on a street, or in an alleyway. It may be attempted near people or out of earshot of people. The conditions will determine your response. In the end, it comes down to difficult choices. A woman who offers no resistance is more likely to be raped and less likely to get hurt. A woman who resists is less likely to be raped but more likely to be hurt. Those are not easy alternatives. On balance, prudence is the course of wisdom. Better to come out of the assault with your life, limbs, and future preserved rather than risk all in hopeless resistance. And, certainly, if the rapist uses a knife or gun, don't fight back. The risks are simply too great. And the fact is that many rapists are armed. One study showed that 43 percent of them used guns, knives, sticks, or other weapons.

The best that you as an older woman can do where rape is concerned is to face the facts calmly. The odds are that you will never have to experience this threat. And you can take the above precautions to reduce significantly the likelihood of your becoming a rape victim. Follow these precautions and give yourself the best odds possible.

Rape Crisis Centers

But suppose it happens? You took every precaution. You were still raped. Now what do you do? Reporting a rape takes courage. Any woman who does so deserves society's gratitude and admiration. The road is not likely to be easy for her, for she enters a sometimes confusing and seemingly insensitive legal bureaucracy.

Nevertheless, rape is the kind of crime that is often committed repeatedly by the same offenders. One frequently reads of a rapist apprehended only after numerous offenses. Consequently, stopping a single rapist can avert many future rapes. And the only way the offender can be stopped is if his crimes are reported.

Few experiences that a woman undergoes can be more devastating than rape and its aftermath. Along with the terror, the victim often experiences guilt. Did she somehow behave in a way that invited the assault? The rape may give her feelings of inferiority. She may wonder why she was singled out for violation. The thought of describing to strangers—to the police—the physical details of what happened is repellent. Many women tend to withdraw, to say nothing, and to endure their suffering in silence and isolation.

Fortunately, there has emerged in recent years a growing recognition of the special psychological and other needs of the rape victim. To meet these needs, more and more communities are establishing rape relief or rape crisis centers. One center varies from another, but generally centers tend to offer common services. The center may provide a twenty-four-hour telephone hot line that rape victims can call for immediate assistance. The center may thereafter provide a qualified counselor to take the victim through the various medical, legal, and investigative steps following the assault. Having a trained, sympathetic person to help at this time can be a great comfort to the distraught, often confused victim. The counselor can break the news to members of the victim's family, which is a painful thing for the victim to have to do. The counselor may arrange to have the police investigators tape the victim's statement so that she does not have to go through the trauma of repeating it again and again.

Above all, the center personnel let rape victims know that they are not alone in their hour of need. The staff understands the assault made on the victim's self-respect along with the physical violation. Staff members can help the victim recover her self-respect and see herself as an innocent victim of a crime that countless other women have also suffered. In short, they can help ease the pain.

Naturally, the time to be aware of the existence of a rape crisis center is before a rape happens. Afterward, the victim may be in no shape to find out. Check now to see if your community offers this service. If so, keep the phone number handy.

Important Evidence

One last thought on this painful subject. Your first reaction upon being raped may be to want to cleanse yourself of the horrible experience. But do not bathe, change clothes, or

douche right away. Report the rape to the police or rape crisis
center first and clean up after the preliminary investigation.
Your physical condition and the condition of your clothes may
become important evidence in convicting the rapist.

Assault

Ted U., sixty-two, was a marine veteran of the campaigns on
Iwo Jima and Okinawa. He had been seriously wounded in
the latter campaign and spent a year in a Veterans Administration hospital. Thereafter, he walked with a slight limp.

Ted considered himself a tough customer. Consequently, when three young hoodlums pulled a knife on Ted
and told him to hand over his money, he took a swing at the
biggest one. He missed, and immediately the robbers wrestled
him to the ground and stabbed him. They took his wallet
and his ring and left him bleeding profusely. Ted barely
escaped with his life and spent a long time convalescing.

Ted U. was a victim of assault. There are two degrees of
assault. Simple assault is defined by the FBI as "the unlawful
intentional inflicting of less than serious bodily injury without a
deadly weapon" or "the attempt to do so." Simple assault, for
instance, is one fan shoving another at a ball game. Aggravated
assault is "the unlawful intentional inflicting of serious bodily
injury or unlawful threat or attempt to inflict bodily injury or
death by means of a deadly or dangerous weapon." Once a
deadly weapon is involved, it is aggravated assault whether or
not injury is done.

Ted was a victim of aggravated assault, which is what
people understandably fear most. Aggravated assault is a common enough crime. According to the National Crime Survey,
about 1.5 million aggravated assaults were committed in 1983.
Still, this crime runs far behind property crimes such as larceny
(23.8 million) or burglary (6 million).

What is the danger of older Americans becoming victims
of aggravated assault? Fortunately, the odds are not too great.
Most aggravated assaults happen to victims between the ages of
sixteen and twenty-four. A person in that group is nine times

more likely to be assaulted seriously than someone aged fifty or older. For every person aged sixty-five or older who is assaulted, at least forty-six persons aged twenty-four or under are assaulted. The difference is explained largely by the life-styles of younger people compared to less active and less risk-taking lifestyles of older people.

Not surprisingly, the likeliest place to be assaulted is in the big city. Victimization rates there are double what they are in small towns or rural areas.

The weapons that assailants use are more or less evenly divided among guns, knives, clubs, fists, and feet.

Preventive Measures to Take

Most assaults grow out of other crimes—interrupted rob-beries, burglaries, and purse snatchings, for example. There-fore, if you take measures to avoid those crimes, you will at the same time reduce the chances of your being assaulted. If the burglar can't get in your house, you don't get beat up in the course of a burglary.

Sometimes the assault is prompted by the victim's resist-ance or slowness to comply with a robber's demands. Don't try to be a hero. Your life is worth more than anything in your pocket. Sometimes the assault results from pure sadism. How-ever, random violence—a senseless, unprovoked beating inflicted on you by an unknown assailant, for example—is the rarest form of aggravated assault.

What to Do If Assaulted

Suppose that you have taken all the precautions against being burglarized, robbed, or raped. You have made your home secure; avoided dark, deserted streets; and parked your car in busy, well-lit places. All this effort may help prevent an assault, but it does not rule it out. What should you do if you are threatened with assault or actually assaulted?

First of all, don't make Ted's mistake. He, consciously or unconsciously, put the question to himself, What's more impor-tant, my pride and possessions or my life? And he came up with the wrong answer. As a result, he almost lost his life. And don't try to make your assailant feel guilty or try to play on his sympathies or try to talk him out of the crime. Don't warn him,

"You could get twenty years for this, buster." Virtually anything that you do apart from handing over what the criminal wants increases the likelihood of his attacking you. Even something as mild as "Take it easy" might trigger a warped personality to turn on you. And don't expect the criminal to be touched by your pleas for sympathy. Your plea is only likely to provoke him further.

When you are faced with someone who can do you bodily harm, set this as your major objective: I want to get out of this situation alive with the least injury possible. So, do as your assailant tells you.

Also, heed what the police experts say about carrying weapons to protect yourself. If you carry a weapon, you are only increasing the risk of serious injury to yourself. If, for example, you start to pull a gun while being robbed, you will likely provoke the criminal to act rashly.

If it appears inevitable that you are still going to be attacked, your next objective should be to try to get away. If that is not possible and you are under attack, holler your head off and defend yourself with whatever you can get your hands on—a rock, a stick, or even a bottle.

If the assault occurs in your home, try to get out. If you can get to a bedroom or bathroom, do so and lock the door. Open the window and yell for help. If you have the time and can reach a phone, call the police.

If your assailant is trying to escape, let him. Don't try to block his way.

Remember your priorities. Save your life first. Worry about anything else second. It is far preferable to end up as a robbery statistic than as an assault or even murder statistic.

Murder Statistics

On the subject of murder, it may be of some consolation to know that the crime dreaded most is least likely to happen to older people. Murder is tragically common in the United States, something like twenty thousand murders per year. Yet, the chances of your becoming a murder victim are about one in ten thousand. If you are older, the odds are even less. In one recent year, only 6 percent of all murder victims were aged sixty-five or older. The likelihood that even these murders were committed by predators preying on strangers was slight. Most murders occur among people who know each other. Murder results commonly from family disputes and flare-ups among friends and acquaintances.

Psychological Problems of Victims

The emphasis in this book has been on preventive techniques, what you can do to lessen the odds of becoming a criminal victim. Some of us are inevitably going to be victimized, the statistics say. These crime victims will face certain psychological problems.

Everyone experiences fear when confronted with crime. Yet people are conditioned to be ashamed of being frightened. They should not be ashamed. Healthy fear is nature's protective mechanism. Fear will make you do things to help you survive danger. Panic, on the other hand, is something else. Panic will paralyze your intelligence. Try not to panic in the course of a crime committed against you. Try to stay as calm as possible. Keep thinking to yourself, What should I do to get out of this in one piece?

After you have been victimized, you are likely to feel anger, outrage, and even shame. But don't be too hard on yourself. Virtually every crime victim goes through the same cycle of emotions. Look at it this way. If you survived a crime with your life saved and as little injury as possible, you handled it well.

Afterward, friends, relatives, and even the police may say insensitive things to you: "Why were you on that street at that hour?" "Don't you know enough to lock your door?" "What were you doing that they picked on you?" However well-intentioned this kind of talk may be, it is nevertheless going to add to your feelings of guilt and lowered self-esteem. Don't let it. The crime didn't happen to them; it happened to you. They are second-guessing. They might have behaved worse as victims. Furthermore, the idea that you somehow "invited" your own victimization is nonsense. Crimes happen. People can reduce them. They cannot prevent all of them.

What the criminal victim needs to hear is simply, "I'm sorry it happened to you. I'm glad you got out of it all right.

And don't blame yourself. It wasn't your fault.'' That is probably as much as you will want to hear if you are a victim. Maybe you didn't take all the precautions you should have. Maybe you will do things differently next time. But the main thing is that you survived. And that is enough for now.

DON'TS AND DOS

Don't

- open your door to strangers.
- resist a rapist in a hopeless situation—when he is armed and threatening and you are isolated from help.
- wash or change clothes if raped until you have reported the crime and the preliminary investigation has taken place.
- accept or give rides to strangers.
- resist a robber, especially an armed one.
- be clever, plead for sympathy, or try to talk yourself out of a robbery. The robbery could become an assault.
- carry a weapon to protect yourself—it's too dangerous.

Do

- list your first initial instead of your first name in the phone book or on your mailbox if you are a woman living alone.
- have a telephone in your bedroom where you can reach it quickly.
- know in advance the number of your local rape crisis center.
- make sure no one is hiding in your car before you get into it.
- deter rapists by keeping your doors and windows locked.
- avoid deserted streets, shortcuts, parks, schoolyards, Laundromats, and laundry rooms at night.
- avoid getting in an elevator with a suspicious male.
- avoid groups of men or boys who are loitering.
- flee a rapist if you can—and do so screaming.
- if you attack a rapist, get the rapist in the eyes or genitals.
- report to the police if you are raped.
- call a rape crisis center if you are raped.
- if assaulted, try first to get away. Fight only if you cannot escape.

9 *Travel Safety*

For Al and Ginny W., it was a dream come true. Al had just retired after thirty years of teaching at Johnstown High School. Ginny had worked for fifteen years as a secretary after the children had grown up and gone off on their own. Al and Ginny wanted to make this two-month, once-in-a-lifetime trip to Europe while they were still young enough to enjoy it. They had watched their pennies these last few years and had saved enough to travel in modest but comfortable style.

For Al, a former world history teacher, Rome had to be the first stop. They had found a nice budget hotel near the Spanish Steps, and they had rented a small Fiat. As soon as they had checked into their room, Al insisted that they make a beeline for the Coliseum.

After getting hopelessly lost, they finally found a parking place near the magnificent ancient amphitheater. They got out of the car, and Al stood there gawking at the Coliseum as though he could not believe that they were really there. Suddenly, they heard glass shattering. They turned to see a young man and a girl speeding off on a motor scooter. The girl was clutching the rider with one arm and holding something blue in the other.

Al thought that maybe the motor scooter had struck a car. Then Ginny gasped. Her hand went to her mouth. Al felt a cold chill. The window on the driver's side of their rented car was broken. Al's blue canvas shoulder bag was gone. In it they had left their airline tickets, their passports, a camera, seven hundred dollars in cash, and fifteen hundred dollars in traveler's checks. The pair on the motor scooter had smashed the window and seized the bag in one swift, practiced maneuver. In an instant, the dream trip had become a nightmare.

Traveling anywhere, at home or abroad, compounds crime problems. Never are you more vulnerable. You find yourself in unfamiliar places, surrounded by strangers, loaded down with baggage, and carrying more money than usual. The situation is even worse abroad. There you may face a language barrier and often baffling foreign customs. And the fact that you are a tourist is not easily concealed to the sharp-eyed operator. To every thief, pickpocket, and con artist, you stand out like an Arab sheikh at a baseball game.

Yet, travel is one of the most exciting and enriching adventures one can experience. Older persons are not about to give it up. Besides, the trip need not be made a treat for the criminal if you take certain precautions.

Predeparture Precautions

Many of the precautions to prevent crime hold true for travel as well. For example, the first step toward a crime-free vacation is to make your home secure while you are gone by following the antiburglary tips from chapter 1. Have the right locks on doors and windows, and lock them. Advise the police and trusted neighbors or friends when you are going, where, and for how long. Get your valuables and money out of the house and into a safe-deposit box or other secure place. Make your house look occupied while you are away.

Here's another wise predeparture precaution. Check your homeowners' insurance policy. Does it provide theft coverage while you are staying in hotels and motels? It should.

Let's assume that you have gone carefully over the Vacation Check-Off List (page 13) and everything is shipshape.

Packing

Now it's time to pack. Make sure that you have locks on your luggage. And when you are done packing, lock the luggage. Locks won't make your bags theft-proof. Since the thief is always looking for the easiest mark, don't make it any easier for him or her by leaving your bags unlocked. Don't overload your luggage either. Overloading can cause luggage to pop open. Luggage lying open in an airline baggage area is all the more tempting for someone with a larcenous streak. Finally, place identification, your name and address, on all your luggage. It is wise to place some identification inside too in case the outside tags get knocked off. If you are flying, don't put cash, checks, and valuables in luggage that you are going to check. Carry those items with you on board. In that way, you are protected both in case of baggage loss or theft.

Now you are ready, indeed eager, to go. But if you are going on a road trip, don't pack your car, camper, or trailer the night before. Loading ahead of time may save a few minutes on your departure day, but a loaded vehicle in the driveway offers thieves a tempting target itself and is an advertisement that you are going to be away.

Cash, Traveler's Checks, and Credit Cards

Do not bring more money on a trip than you need. Take the necessary minimum in cash and buy traveler's checks. Make sure that you keep that slip with the serial numbers of the traveler's checks apart from the checks themselves. While you are at it, write down other important numbers, such as your passport and credit card numbers, and keep the record in a safe, accessible place.

It is advisable to use credit cards when you travel. Major credit cards are accepted not only at home but also in cities throughout the world. In addition, certain credit card companies will let you cash personal checks with your card. This service allows you to reduce the amount of cash and traveler's checks that you have to bring with you, and that means less money to be lost or stolen. When using a credit card, make certain the card returned by the clerk after the purchase is your card and not a "hot," or stolen, one.

e a few more room precautions. You might want to
ber wedge in the space between the floor and the
e door. The wedge will prevent the door from being
. And, after you're done admiring the breathtaking
bacabana Beach or Sun Valley, make sure that the
door to your balcony is locked. Also, put some-
tracks to keep a burglar from sliding the glass door

ne knocks at your door, make the person identify
erself first before you open the door. If you did not
service, the laundry, or a bellhop, or whoever the
to be, check the front desk for verification.

nd Elevators

lnerable places for guests in hotels and motels are
indoor garages, and corridors. If you see anyone
rking in those areas, alert the hotel security staff.
or wander about unnecessarily in corridors. That is
likely to be accosted. Find the most direct route
om to the elevator or stairway and always use it.
nly good fire-safety advice but also an anticrime

el uneasy about someone who is about to get on
vith you and you are alone, don't get on. If it's too
nal your intentions by pushing your floor number.
go back to the lobby and start over. Stand close to
nel, where you can reach the emergency button if

hese precautions so that when friends wish you a
can expect to have one.

Cabdrivers

One of the commonest travel mishaps is experienced by the new
arrival who gets clipped by a dishonest cabdriver on the ride
into town from the airport. We've all heard of the flustered
foreigner who is informed by an unscrupulous cabbie that his
ride in from JFK airport to Manhattan costs $175. It happens all
over the world. The best precaution is to ask the driver *in
advance* how much the ride is going to cost.

Safeguarding Valuables

So far, you have made it from home to your hotel or motel.
When checking into your accommodations, try to avoid rooms
on the ground floor or even upper-level rooms that appear easily
accessible to intruders. And use the hotel or motel safe-deposit
service. Put your jewelry and other valuables in the box, along
with important documents like your passport. Also leave
unneeded cash and traveler's checks in the safe-deposit box.
Again, the commonsense rule is to never carry on you more
money than you can afford to lose.

The precaution not to carry all the money on you in one
place is obviously even more important when you travel
because you usually have more money with you. That was the
mistake that Al and Ginny W. made. They had used the shoulder bag for most of their valuables. A money belt is an excellent
safeguard when you travel. Divide your money among wallets,
purses, pockets, and the money belt. If a thief is going to snatch
your basket, don't have all your eggs in it.

If you are traveling abroad and your passport is stolen,
report the loss to the nearest American embassy or consulate. It
is a good idea also to carry a valid copy of your birth certificate
on the trip. The birth certificate will make it easier for you to
have a new passport issued.

Car Security

The car security precautions you take at home are even more
important when you travel. Again, you are more likely to have
valuable items inside the car when you travel. Also, it is much
more complicated and unnerving to deal with thefts in places

where you are a stranger. Roll up the windows and lock the car when you park. And avoid parking in poorly lit and lightly traveled streets. Keep packages out of sight, locked up in the trunk. Never leave items of value on the car seat when you get out, not for an instant. Thieves have well-rehearsed routines. The tourist simply has to be doubly alert. You are the favorite target of every crook seeking victims with that just-off-the-plane look.

When traveling in cities new to you, particularly foreign cities, be especially careful to avoid questionable neighborhoods, suspicious persons, and dark streets.

When you arrive at your lodgings, even if for one night, don't leave luggage in the car overnight. Bring it into your room.

Sensible Sight-seeing

Do your sight-seeing sensibly. You are better off getting tour advice from a hotel desk clerk, a professional travel agent, or an accredited guide, rather than from a cabdriver or waiter. See those intriguing, out-of-the-way places during the daytime. And, if you want to go out on the town at night, do so with a group.

Exchange "Bargains"?

Suppose you are abroad and somebody on the street offers you a much higher exchange rate for your dollars than you have been quoted by your hotel or commercial exchange. Watch out! First of all, if you accept, you may be violating the country's currency laws. Secondly, more than one greedy tourist has wound up with a wad of worthless paper instead of lire, francs, or marks. And, finally, the exchange "bargain" may be a trick to lure you to an unsafe place for a robbery.

Room Security

Assume that you have been careful. You've had a great day riding the Grand Canyon on a mule or tramping through the Louvre. You are back in your hotel or motel room. Robberies

Here a
insert a rub
bottom of th
forced open
view of Co
sliding glass
thing in the
open.

If anyo
himself or h
ask for room
caller claims

Corridors a

The most vu
parking lots,
suspicious lu
Don't linger
where you a
from your ro
That is not o
precaution.

If you f
the elevator v
late, don't sig
It is better to
the control pa
you have to.

Follow t
safe trip, you

and burglaries in these plac
tions should you take? I
spring-latch locks. They a
kind that lock automatical
are a cinch for thieves to
rooms will also have dead
turn manually, and chain
the locks that you find in h
portable travel lock with
door. Portable locks are
smiths. See figure 1.

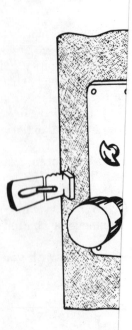

Fi

DON'TS AND DOS

Don't

- pack your car or other vehicle the night before you leave.
- overload your luggage. It may pop open.
- pack cash or valuables in luggage to be checked.
- carry more cash on you than you can afford to lose.
- take a hotel or motel room on the first floor if avoidable.
- leave cash or valuables in the room.
- admit unidentified persons into your room.
- get on an elevator alone with a suspicious person.
- change money on the street in foreign countries.

Do

- check your homeowners' policy for hotel and motel coverage before you travel.
- purchase traveler's checks and use credit cards.
- write down numbers of credit cards and passports and keep the record in a safe place.
- put identification inside and outside of your luggage.
- ask the cabdriver in advance what the ride from the airport into town will cost.
- use a hotel's safe-deposit box for your money, valuables, and important papers.
- follow all car-safety precautions. Roll up windows, lock doors, and park in safe places.
- bring your luggage into your room at night.
- use a money belt. Divide money and traveler's checks between pockets, wallets, purses, and the belt.
- carry a valid copy of your birth certificate.

10 *Neighborhood Efforts Against Crime*

Laurence A., a retired air force officer, and his wife, Estelle, a schoolteacher, lived on Jordan Road in a Washington, D.C., suburb. Moving vans were not an uncommon sight in their neighborhood because people were so often being transferred in and out of the capital area. Ordinarily, Laurence would not have given this van a second thought as he walked to a nearby shopping center to pick up a newspaper. Two young men were carrying a television set out of a house into the van. He could see some other furniture already loaded into it. The van was a rental vehicle, and Laurence became suspicious because he did not recognize the people loading it.

As he passed by the van, Laurence said, "I see the Franklins are moving back to Florida." Actually, he knew that the family came from New York.

The man gave him a fish-eyed look and muttered, "Yeh."

Laurence was instantly on guard but kept on walking. Almost immediately, the two men hopped into the car of the van and sped away. Laurence noted the license plate, ran back to his house, called the police, and told them what he had observed.

Within twenty minutes, the police apprehended the two men in the van. They were burglars, cleaning out the house while the Franklins were off on a vacation.

What had made Laurence A. vigilant was the fact that he had recently joined the Springfield Neighborhood Watch Association. Through this organization, he had learned how ordinary citizens, banded together, can prevent crimes. Police forces alone can do little to prevent most crimes. The police will be the first to agree. They largely react to crimes already committed. No reasonable person is suggesting that ordinary citizens take the law into their own hands or advocating that gun-toting vigilantes deal with crime. But there are several safe, sensible citizen initiatives to stop crime that require no money, are easy to organize, and demand little time.

Volunteer cooperative effort represents the American way. From the beginning, Americans have been characterized by voluntarily banding together to tackle common problems. The pioneer forebears settled the continent largely through reliance and dependence on one another. In the early days of the Republic, there was no police protection in the modern sense. Private citizens did the job. In Boston and New York, for example, "citizen watches" provided protection. These watches were appointed by local officials to walk the streets at night. The watchers carried bells or other noisemakers to alert people in case of fires, public disorders, or thievery. In New York, the watchers carried rattles and were called the Rattle Watch. Early watchers were not even paid for their services. Finally, in 1801, Boston started paying its citizen watchdogs fifty cents a night. There are now modern descendants of those Rattle Watches and bell ringers.

Neighborhood Watch

A Seattle, Washington, survey showed that citizens in that city worried more about burglary than any other crime. Most of the city's burglaries, the police found, were made through unlocked doors and windows in homes. And most burglaries occurred during daylight.

Seattle's citizens and police got together to deal with the problem. The police helped organize "neighborhood watches" in various parts of the city. At these gatherings, people were instructed in antiburglary fundamentals, and they banded together for joint action. They were organized into teams of ten to twenty households to look after one another's homes.

In Seattle, the neighborhood watch program resulted in a decline in burglaries ranging from 48 to 61 percent in various parts of the city.

You can form a neighborhood watch organization where you live. First, find out who is the crime-prevention officer in your local police department or sheriff's office. You will find that most law-enforcement agencies are geared up for and eager to provide this assistance. The police like to have citizens realize how much they themselves can do to prevent crime.

The next step is to get the word out to your neighbors that a neighborhood watch organization is being considered. Again, the police will be happy to help stage the initial organizing meeting. A police crime-prevention officer may likely begin by giving a profile of crime in your neighborhood. You will learn just how many burglaries are actually committed and the burglars' methods of operation in your area. You may even experience a certain amount of relief to find that the crimes you dread most are the least likely to be committed. For instance, you may learn that while burglaries and youthful vandalism are frequent, muggings, rapes, and assaults are rare. You may be stunned to learn how many of your neighbors have been bilked by con artists.

After giving your group a neighborhood crime profile, the officer will then likely cover burglary-prevention techniques that you should adopt in your own home. He or she may also show a film on the subject. But, at the heart of the neighborhood watch program is surveillance, and the crime-prevention officer will instruct your group in surveillance techniques for reporting crime and suspicious persons or occurrences. The officer can tell you how to organize your neighborhood watch into groups of families, each of which agrees to look out for the others' homes, especially when someone is away.

Here are the kinds of things that the police suggest you report to them under a neighborhood watch program.

– "Lost" individuals appearing at your door.

– Any repair people coming to your door when you have not called for service.

- A stranger in the neighborhood carrying household items such as a stereo or television set to a truck or car.

- Strangers loitering around your neighbor's house, particularly if the neighbor is away.

- Unknown drivers cruising the neighborhood for no apparent reason.

- Broken or open windows and doors.

- Persons walking the street and peering into parked cars.

- Someone removing parts from a car—such as the radio, tape deck, batteries, or license plate—especially if you doubt that the person is the owner.

You should also report screams or other sounds of someone in distress and loud, unusual noises or explosions.

Mutual surveillance is critical to the neighborhood watch program. It's the modern version of the pioneer spirit—people looking out for one another.

Feedback is essential to a successful neighborhood watch. You want to know what effect your efforts are having on crime. A decline in burglaries tells you that the system is working and encourages people to keep up the good work. Or, you and your neighbors may learn that only parts of the program are working. Maybe burglar entries through front doors and windows have declined, but entries through unlocked back doors have gone up. At least now you know where to concentrate your efforts next. Neighborhood watch gets the highest endorsement. Imprisoned burglars questioned by criminologists say that they would leave a neighborhood where they knew that they were being watched or where people challenged what they were doing there.

Citizen Patrols

Sun City, Arizona, is a retirement community about twenty miles northwest of Phoenix. Some years ago, this town of thirty thousand was suffering a rash of vandalism, pilferage, and burglaries. Sun City was an easy mark for every junkie in the area looking for somebody to rip off to finance the next fix.

The Maricopa County Sheriff's Department had a tough time protecting the area—with only three patrol cars to cover a community of ten thousand acres, including seven shopping centers. Consequently, Sun City's citizens did what their pioneer ancestors did when they faced a common danger. They banded together for mutual assistance and formed the Sun City Posse.

Today, the Sun City Posse numbers about 250 men and women. They do not carry weapons or string up the bad guys, but they do prevent crime. The posse members, distinguishable by their white hard-hat helmets, are divided into two-person teams. They carry only whistles and flashlights. Through community donations, they are also equipped with mobile radio communications, allowing them to be in touch with the county sheriff's department and the Phoenix police force. Each team patrols a sector of Sun City in an unmarked car. These teams cover the city day and night. They look for anything suspicious or unusual. When they spot something odd, they radio the police. For example, one posse patrol reported a man busily pruning shrubs and raking the lawn around a house while the owners were away. The posse's suspicions brought out the sheriff's deputies, who found a second man inside ransacking the house.

Not long after the Sun City Posse was formed, the city achieved the lowest burglary rate of any large community in the county.

In Manatee County, Florida, a trailer park was plagued by teenagers from surrounding areas who seemed to think, as one resident put it, "we were a bunch of old, defenseless people." The park residents got together and formed a community security patrol. They got help and cooperation from the sheriff's office. As a result, break-ins and vandalism were reduced. And now, says the same resident, "The atmosphere after dark has changed completely for the better."

Not all citizen patrols succeed. In order for a citizen patrol to work, it must have the full support and cooperation of local government officials and enforcement agencies. Without this support, citizen patrols lack the professional backup required for success.

If you want to start a citizen patrol in your area, begin by contacting your local law-enforcement people to help you. Clearly identify your problems to them. Then develop a sensible, cooperative allocation of responsibilities between the citizen patrol and the professionals. If the police are in your corner and you each know your part in the patrol, you are off to a good start.

The duties of the citizen patrol should match the nature of the problem. If, for example, women in your community are being harassed while coming home at night, you will want to concentrate the patrol where and when the trouble occurs. The problem might be between four and eight in the evening on a street running from a bus stop to a housing project. The point is to identify the problem clearly, make a plan to meet it, and make sure that you have the involvement and cooperation of the police right from the start.

Crime Stoppers

Several communities have found "tip" programs like Crime Stoppers a highly effective citizen-involvement technique for solving crimes. In the Washington, D.C., Crime Stoppers' program, the police urge the public to help solve "the crime of the week," which is publicized on television. People possessing information about the crime are asked to call the police. The call and the caller's identity are kept confidential. The Crime Stoppers' program has opened up numerous otherwise dead-end cases—the murder of a retired couple, for example, that had failed to produce a logical suspect and the death of a young girl in a clueless case. Police in the nation's capital credit Crime Stoppers with a major role in that city's substantial decline in violent crime in recent months.

Neighborhood Crime Prevention

Community cooperation need not be as formalized as a neighborhood watch or Crime Stoppers to be successful. Take the case of a retirement community that was plagued by vandalism. The neighbors got together and called the police to explain their problem. They and the police devised a simple strategy. The residents whose homes bordered the park agreed to leave their outside lights on all night long. They learned that this would cost only a few pennies a night. For their part, the police agreed to send a patrol car through the community several times each night. That was all. Nothing further was done. The vandalism stopped.

Another simple crime-stopper is the buddy system. It's a neighborhood watch on the smallest scale. You and a neighbor simply agree to look out for each other. It's, "I'll watch your house while you're away, and you watch mine when I go." Similarly, older persons may agree that they will always go out shopping or run errands together. Another buddy system tactic involves the telephone check. The two parties agree to check up on each other by telephone every day at about the same time to make sure everything is in order.

Here's another example of simple, effective community action. Residents in a neighborhood of row houses in a large eastern city were experiencing muggings, assaults, burglaries, and harassment of older women. They got together at a block party one night and decided to do something to protect themselves. They did not start a formal neighborhood watch organization, but they did all agree to do certain things. They agreed to keep an eye on strangers and report anything suspicious to the police. They agreed to take down the license numbers of suspicious cars cruising the block, and they agreed to carry whistles at night.

Those were simple procedures involving little time or effort, but they paid off. For instance, within three weeks, a person who had participated in the block party saw someone lurking in an alley and tipped off the police. A burglar was nabbed. On another night, a car carrying two men slowed down alongside a woman walking from the bus stop to her home. She blew her whistle, and within seconds several residents came out of their houses. The car sped off.

Security Inspection Teams

Older persons and retirees often put their accumulated skills and spare time to good use through volunteer work. One such effort that leads to reduced crime rates is the volunteer security inspection team.

Security inspection teams are made up of people who learn from law-enforcement professionals what has to be done to safeguard homes from burglars. The teams, for example, will notify you and your neighbors, perhaps by phone or handbill, that they are available to check out your house and determine how secure it is. A security inspection team will check the locks on your doors and windows; sliding glass doors; openings into your house through the basement, vents, windows, garage, and roof; and your disposition of house keys. They will check to see if utility poles and trees are undesirably close to your windows. They will note whether your ladders are too easily available to a resourceful burglar. Then they will tell you what you need to do to make your house more secure. They will work from a checklist similar to the one on page 130.

A common problem that people have in making their homes more burglarproof is knowing where to find people to do the work required, such as changing from spring-latch to dead-bolt locks. Security inspection teams often have a roster of persons available for such jobs. And they can guide you to locksmiths, alarm companies, and hardware dealers who can help. If you want to start a security inspection team in your neighborhood, the place to call is the crime-prevention unit of your police department or sheriff's office. They will be glad to help. In some communities, your police department may itself provide a security inspection service.

Alarm and Hardware Committees

You and your neighbors may want to form an alarm and hardware team either as part of or separate from a security inspection team. There are all kinds of alarm devices on the market today. The sheer number and their different capabilities, prices, and purposes can easily bewilder the lay person. You can find systems that turn on lights; sound an audible alarm; transmit a silent alarm; or automatically dial certain phone numbers giving a prerecorded message, for example, to your doctor or son or daughter. There are alarms that link you to the police and alarms that photograph a protected area, the kind you have seen in banks.

This array can be confusing. Almost every neighborhood

HOME SECURITY CHECK-OFF LIST

	Yes	No
1. Have your doors, windows, and other openings been inspected to determine if the locking devices are secure?		
2. When you leave the house vacant, do you always lock the doors and windows?		
3. Does the house look ''lived in'' during your absence?		
4. Do you leave several lights on when you are absent during the evening?		
5. Are ladders secured and out of sight?		
6. Are valuable wheeled items, such as bicycles and lawn mowers, out of sight and secured?		
7. Do you hide your house keys under flowerpots, in the mailbox, or under doormats?		
8. Do you leave notes on your door when you are out?		
9. Do you have a safe-deposit box for securing valuables?		
10. Have you devised methods whereby only very small amounts of money are kept in the house?		
11. Do you lock up your checkbook?		
12. Have you made a record of credit cards or other papers that can be identified by number?		
13. Have you marked your most vulnerable property with your personal ID mark?		
14. Have you inventoried and recorded your valuables?		
15. Are utility poles and trees undesirably close to your windows?		

has its gifted do-it-yourselfers—people who are handy and comfortable with gadgetry and tools—and there will likely be an engineer or two on your block. These neighbors make excellent members of an alarm and hardware team, since many of them find the subject fascinating.

An alarm and hardware team familiarizes itself with the equipment available—what it does, where it can be purchased, what is involved in installation, and what it costs. The team then makes itself available to come to your home to advise you as to which alarms you may want, need, and can afford.

Property Identification

Another project that can be worked out between citizen volunteers and local law-enforcement officials is the property identification program. Under this program, small electric etching tools are made available so that people can mark their property with their names, initials, or an identifying number. Branded cattle are less likely to be rustled, and so are your possessions.

Public Lighting

Crime is one pernicious weed that does not thrive in the light. Proper lighting can make your home less crime-prone. Good public lighting provides many advantages as well as greater security from nighttime crime. Good lighting improves roadway safety and cuts down on pedestrian accidents. Business does better in well-lighted areas.

In many cities, people have organized to have their street lighting improved. If you believe that your community can benefit from better lighting, talk to your neighbors about mounting an improved-lighting campaign. It may take a while. You will have to educate and motivate your neighbors, and, eventually, you will have to win over your public officials. But you should not have much trouble in enlisting the local police chief in your cause. The chief knows that crime thrives in darkness. Bring your local power company into the picture. Company representatives can provide the expertise on systems, equipment, and costs involved. They have an obvious interest in better lighting.

There are numerous examples of citizen movements that have led to better-lighting campaigns—and reduced crime. A small rural women's club in one state started a lighting campaign. In time, the movement spread throughout the state.

Publicity

Whatever the citizen crime-fighting initiative that you want to explore, you will likely find your local news media ready to help with publicity. Newspapers and radio and television stations are happy to publicize volunteer organizations with good community programs. These efforts alert criminals that your neighborhood is no longer going to be a sitting duck.

DON'TS AND DOS

Don't

- accept the notion that your community has to take crime lying down.
- be paralyzed by hopelessness, fear, or inertia into inaction. Apathy did not build this country.
- expect the police to provide you with complete protection.

Do

- band together with your neighbors in citizen crime-reduction efforts.
- look out for one another.
- confront crime with the power of united, determined people.

11 *Good Citizenship and Good Sense*

Amelia H., fifty-seven, divorced, lived on the second floor of an apartment house on Euclid Avenue in a midwestern city. She had just returned home from her nearby public library with Barbara Cartland's latest novel when she heard a scream down the hall—just one sharp cry, then nothing more. Several thoughts raced through Amelia's mind at once. First, there had been several rapes in the neighborhood over the past months. Still, she could not assume that a scream meant a crime. A different breed of tenants had been moving into her building lately, and fights and shouting at all hours had become common. Amelia had no desire to get herself involved in other people's quarrels. She had enough troubles of her own.

Still, Amelia had always been haunted by the story of the young woman, years before, who had been brutally stabbed to death in New York City while over thirty of her neighbors heard her screams but never called the police—the Kitty Genovese case. So, when she heard a second scream, Amelia decided to do something. She opened her door a crack and peered down the hallway. Just as she did, a man came out of an apartment and hurried in her direction. Then he headed down the center stairway. Amelia got a good look at him. She had never seen the man before, but then again, there were so many new people in the building now.

133

Amelia's heart was pounding. She closed the door and thought for a few minutes. What kind of world would it be, she wondered, if everybody closed their eyes and shut their ears to unpleasantness that didn't affect them directly? Maybe the man was there legitimately. But maybe he had hurt someone who now needed help. Amelia went to her telephone and called the police.

It was well that she did. The police came immediately and found a woman semiconscious in the apartment down the hall. She had been raped and badly beaten.

Fortunately, Amelia H. proved sharp-eyed. She gave the police a good description of the man she had seen. In fact, she had picked up one detail that even his terrified victim had failed to notice. Under his jacket, the man had on a pale green top, the kind worn by hospital orderlies. With that clue, the police tracked down the assailant at the general hospital where he worked. He was arrested and charged with rape and aggravated assault.

Months later Amelia H. was called as a witness at the trial. She found the whole business upsetting and sometimes wondered whether she had done the smart thing in getting herself involved.

On the stand, the victim proved to be a hazy witness. She had been so traumatized by the experience that she had failed to remember much about the rapist. Amelia's testimony, consequently, proved critical. The defendant was convicted and sentenced to ten years in the penitentiary.

After the trial, the district attorney thanked Amelia for her cooperation. He informed her that the rapist had committed an average of three assaults a month for the preceding six months. Amelia could credit herself with potentially saving dozens of women from this trauma by helping put the criminal away. One of the spared victims, he pointed out, might well have been herself.

You, as an individual, can do many things to prevent crime. You cannot rely solely on law-enforcement agencies to protect you. There simply are not enough police to control the volume of crime in this country. Police forces largely have their hands full just keeping up with crimes already committed. But once a crime has been committed, or you think it has, your cooperation with law-enforcement authorities is absolutely essential if criminals are to be brought to justice.

Few criminals stop at a single offense. Consequently, the conviction and imprisonment of criminals is vital to the reduction of future crime. As a responsible citizen, you can and should do certain things to help the authorities apprehend criminals and thus make your community and yourself safer.

Ironically, people will not hesitate to report a fire, but they are much less likely to report a crime. Fire departments, for example, are constantly getting called to investigate evidence of smoke (it may turn out to be somebody illicitly burning trash, but better safe than sorry). Yet, according to experts, something like half of the crimes committed in this country go unreported. Is there less urgency in reporting that someone may be being robbed or beaten to death than that smoke is coming out of someone's backyard? Naturally, the police don't want to encourage frivolous calls, but if you think that something looks suspicious, the police want you to inform them. They cannot investigate crimes that they don't know about.

Research shows that the sooner a crime is reported, the more likely the culprit is to be caught. A crime reported within two minutes is far more likely to be solved than one reported in two hours. Nor can prosecutors build cases without witnesses and evidence. The only way to prevent others, or yourself, from future victimization is to help the authorities catch criminals now.

It is also in your self-interest to report crimes, even if they aren't solved. You will have better luck with insurance claims, for example, if you can point to an official police report made immediately after a burglary, which cites what you lost. Trying to claim losses from an unreported crime long after the fact is far less convincing to your insurance company.

Reporting to the Police

Amelia H. did not actually witness a crime. She did witness suspicious behavior and wisely reported it. Laurence A. saw men loading furniture from a neighbor's house into a rental van. They could have been on the level, but Laurence became suspicious. He reported the incident to the police, and two burglars were nabbed. The police would far rather run down a lead that turns out to be mistaken than have a real crime go unreported. Your responsibility to your community, your family, *and to yourself* is to report suspicious behavior.

When you do call the police to report something unusual, be calm and factual about it. Begin by identifying yourself. Give your address and phone number. If, for some reason, you are reluctant to identify yourself, call anyway and tell everything you can about the incident that raised your suspicions. Strive for detail. For example, here's what Amelia told the police: "Hello, this is Mrs. Hernandez. I live at the Colony Apartments, 1138 Euclid Avenue, second floor. I just heard screams down the hall. I looked out my door and saw a stranger coming down the hallway in a hurry. He looked to be about twenty, maybe five feet five with reddish hair. I think he was wearing one of those green hospital tops."

Amelia also did the right thing by not trying to handle the situation herself. She did not accost the stranger to ask who he was or what he was doing in the building. That action might have provoked harm to herself. Heroics are not required. Just inform the police and let them take it from there.

Victim and Witness Reports

Roger I., sixty-two, ran a gas station near the Hawk Street viaduct. It was a tough business requiring long, late hours. A till with cash in it provided a tempting target for robbery. Roger accepted the risk almost as part of doing business. The first time he had been robbed, he reported it to the police. Nothing came of the matter—no arrests and certainly no recovery of his money. Two years later, he had been robbed again. This time he did not bother to report the crime. He had lost only a hundred dollars and certainly never expected to see it again. But, two nights later, when the same robber hit him again, Roger called the police. He finally realized that if everybody took crime sitting down, there would be no end to victimization.

In this case the robber was caught because Roger I. gave the police a good description of the getaway car, including the fact that it was burning oil. The police spotted a car of that description, with the telltale fumes, a day later.

Detail is the key to useful identification. The more specific the better. Naturally, someone being robbed, beaten, or raped is not in the best frame of mind for clear thinking. Still, if you are the victim or if you witness a crime, try to be observant. Let your eyes film like a camera and your ears work like a tape recorder.

The principal facts that the police will want to know are these: The sex of the criminal. Approximate age. The build—thin, heavy, medium. Height. In estimating height, use your own eye level as a guide. If you and the criminal are eye to eye, you are about the same height. If you are looking at a person's Adam's apple, add a few inches to your own height. Note the racial or ethnic appearance of the person—white, black, Asian, Hispanic, native American.

Try to note the hair—color, style, and length. Did the criminal have a beard? a moustache? What color were his or her eyes? Did he or she wear glasses? Take note of clothing. Was a hat worn? What kind? A jacket? A suit? Jeans? A shirt? A tie? Boots? Sandals? Running shoes? What was the condition of the clothes—old and dirty or new and neat? Report as much detail as you can remember.

Try particularly to remember anything unusual. Did the person have an accent? speak a foreign language? Was the voice high-pitched or low? Was there a speech impediment? Were distinctive expressions or nicknames used? Did you notice scars, birthmarks, or tattoos? Did the person walk with a limp? have a deformity? have missing teeth? What you are doing is supplying pieces to a jigsaw puzzle that the police are trying to put together. Every piece helps. Don't rely on your memory. Write down everything you can remember as soon as possible.

If a vehicle is involved in the crime, try to be equally specific in your description. What kind of vehicle was it? A sedan? Van? Pickup truck? A big car? A compact? Do you know the make, model, and year? Was it two-door or four-door? The color? Did it have an antenna? Were there significant dents or scratches that you recall? Did it have a vinyl top or rims? If a van, did it have pinstripes, magnesium wheels, or murals on it? Above all, try to get the license number. At least try to remember as much of it as you can. Notice what state the plate is from, even the colors of the plate. Again, write down whatever you have observed as soon as you can. (An easy way to remember a vehicle is to think of the word *CYM-BAL: C,* Color; *Y,* Year; *M,* Make; *B,* Body; *A,* Antenna; *L,* License.)

If others witnessed the crime, ask them for their names and addresses. They may balk, as people often do about getting involved. It might help to remind them that the next victim, if the criminal goes unapprehended, could be one of them.

When the police come, get the investigating officer's name and badge number. You may need it to add further details that come to you later, or you may have questions.

Your Day in Court

If you are a crime victim or a witness, your first exposure to the criminal justice system may be a shock. You will probably be unpleasantly surprised by the bureaucratic, impersonal, sometimes insensitive nature of the system. And you will learn that the wheels of American justice grind exceedingly slow and none too efficiently. Still, it is the only system Americans have and the only means of getting dangerous people off the street and into custody. So do your part to make it work.

First of all, remember that justice does not simply happen. Criminal indictments happen because someone presses charges. Hence the importance again of reporting crime.

Assume that you were a crime victim, your case has been brought to trial, and you have been called as a witness. What can you expect? On your arrival at the courthouse, you may be surprised to find yourself face-to-face with your assailant. It is wise to avoid any confrontation with defendants, members of their families, or their friends. It is possible that they will threaten or otherwise try to intimidate you, even in the halls of justice. Should this happen, report it at once to the prosecutor. Also, report threats that you receive on the street or over the telephone relating to your appearance in a trial.

Be prepared for exasperating delays. American criminal cases take unconscionably long to come to trial—anywhere from a year or longer is not at all unusual. That's why it is important for you to write down the facts of a criminal incident at the time it happens. Memories can be highly unreliable.

If called as a witness, you must appear, even though this may mean time lost from your job or interference with other activities. Once you get to court, you may experience several delays and postponements, which means that you will have to come back again. It seems unfair, and it is aggravating. But that's the present legal system, which could certainly use an overhaul.

How to Be a Good Witness

Being a witness in a criminal case can be an intimidating experience for the unprepared. Yet, the entire case depends on the accumulated evidence that you and other witnesses provide. So your testimony is important. Here are some basic rules to follow to help you be the best witness possible.

Your manner is critical. By being calm, direct, and factual in your responses, you will make a credible witness. Answer all questions in a voice clear enough and loud enough to be heard easily. Stick to the facts and don't stray into the area of opinion. Theorizing will only raise objections and weaken your credibility. Tell the truth. You are under oath. Toying with the facts could expose you to a charge of perjury.

If you do not understand a question, ask that it be repeated or be further explained. Take your time. Do not answer until you know what you are being asked.

Of course, opposing counsel is going to try to shake your story. The defense may try to rattle you. Stay cool. Retain your composure. Don't lose your temper, even if the questions seem deliberately provocative and unfair. If you do, you'll be playing into the opposition's hands. Stick to what you know about what you've been asked. Don't be led afield. Don't argue with opposing counsel. Don't try to be clever, witty, or funny. Lawyers spend years in law school and the courts honing their talents; don't try to outperform them. Your only weapon is the truth, delivered in a direct, factual way.

Victim's Compensation

Over the past few years, a changed atmosphere toward crime in this country has occurred. One benefit of this new climate is more concern for crime victims. Several states have enacted compensation laws for crime victims. If as a result of crime you incur medical expenses, lose income, or suffer property damage, you may be eligible for compensation from the state. These programs vary from state to state, so if you are a crime victim and experience losses as a result, find out if your state has a victim compensation program. As a general rule, it is not necessary that the offender be convicted in order for you to be compensated.

Role of Private Citizen

If criminals are to be punished and kept from committing more crimes, private citizens have roles to perform, along with the authorities. They have a responsibility to report crime, to help the police identify criminals, and to be effective witnesses in court against offenders. Only crimes reported have any chance of being solved; only criminals convicted and isolated can be stopped from perpetrating more crimes. All citizens have a civic duty and a self-interest in this business.

DON'TS AND DOS

Don't
- expect the police to solve crimes without your help.
- try to investigate the crime yourself. Leave that to the police.
- expect the criminal justice process to run quickly or smoothly.
- be an angry, smart-alecky, or disrespectful trial witness.

Do

- report all suspicious persons or events to the police.
- report crimes to the police.
- be as specific as possible in describing persons, vehicles, and events to the police.
- write down immediately what you observe.
- try to get the names and addresses of other witnesses to a crime.
- avoid contact with the defendant and his or her relatives or friends at a trial.
- report threats made against you to the prosecution.
- speak calmly, factually, and to the point as a witness.
- in court, make sure that you understand questions before you answer them.
- if victimized, check to find out if you may be eligible for a compensation program in your state.

A Final Word

One's later years may in some respects seem a time of increasing vulnerability. This is particularly true where health and finances are involved. Another concern that may add to the anxiety of aging is a feeling that older persons are more susceptible to crime, easier targets of the criminals who exploit society. But it has never been the tradition of most Americans, as individuals or as a nation, to take a threat lying down. The approach has been to respond to challenges with courage and intelligence. The fact that one is growing older and living in a crime-plagued society need not change that tradition.

The message of this book is therefore positive. You, as an older person, can be much safer from crime if you know the appropriate crime-fighting precautions and follow them. The theme of this book is simply this: Be aware of the nature of the crime. Anticipate the behavior of the criminal. Take actions that will thwart his or her purpose.

Is this response 100 percent foolproof? Of course not. But the *improvement* that you can achieve in making your life safer from crime can be extraordinary.

Of course, the police are expected to do all they can to prevent and solve crimes. But the police alone cannot remove the threat of crime entirely or even substantially. But you can, in a great measure, lower the odds of becoming a criminal victim. Certain crime threats—burglary, purse snatching, thefts from your car, and most frauds—can virtually be eliminated if you follow the precautions recommended here. In the case of crimes of violence, you can measurably reduce their likelihood and potential injury to yourself by following the advice given in this book.

143

Index

About the Authors

J. E. Persico primarily writes history and biography and is the author of three such works as well as two novels. He is also a frequent contributor to *American Heritage* and other magazines. He has a keen interest in criminal justice, particularly in what the lay person can do to avoid crime. Mr. Persico has served in the U.S. diplomatic corps and as a writer for two governors of New York State, Averell Harriman and Nelson A. Rockefeller. He is a graduate of the State University of New York at Albany and studied at Columbia University Graduate School.